Where 20 or 30
Are Gathered

The Vital Worship, Healthy Congregations Series

John D. Witvliet, Series Editor

Published by the Alban Institute in cooperation with the
Calvin Institute of Christian Worship

BOOKS IN THE SERIES

C. Michael Hawn
One Bread, One Body:
Exploring Cultural Diversity in Worship

Norma deWaal Malefyt and Howard Vanderwell
Designing Worship Together:
Models and Strategies for Worship Planning

Craig A. Satterlee
When God Speaks through Change:
Preaching in Times of Congregational Transition

Peter Bush and Christine O'Reilly
Where 20 or 30 Are Gathered:
Leading Worship in the Small Church

Where 20 or 30 Are Gathered

LEADING WORSHIP IN THE SMALL CHURCH

Peter Bush
Christine O'Reilly

THE ALBAN INSTITUTE

Herndon, Virginia
www.alban.org

The Alban Institute
2121 Cooperative Way, Suite 100
Herndon, VA 20171

Cover design by Adele Robey, Phoenix Graphics.

Library of Congress Cataloging-in-Publication Data

Bush, Peter George, 1962-
   Where 20 or 30 are gathered : leading worship in the small church / Peter G. Bush and H. Christine O'Reilly.
      p. cm. — (Vital worship, healthy congregations series)
   Includes bibliographical references.
   ISBN-13: 978-1-56699-322-7
   ISBN-10: 1-56699-322-9
   1. Small churches. 2. Public worship. I. O'Reilly, H. Christine. II. Title.

BV637.8.B89 2006
264—dc22
                              2005036032

   10   09   08   07   06   VG   1   2   3   4   5

CONTENTS

113691

EDITOR'S FOREWORD

Healthy Congregations

Christianity is a "first-person plural" religion, where communal worship, service, fellowship, and learning are indispensable for grounding and forming individual faith. The strength of Christianity in North America depends on the presence of healthy, spiritually nourishing, well-functioning congregations. Congregations are the cradle of Christian faith, the communities in which children of all ages are supported, encouraged, and formed for lives of service. Congregations are the habitat in which the practices of the Christian life can flourish.

As living organisms, congregations are by definition in a constant state of change. Whether the changes are in membership, pastoral leadership, lay leadership, the needs of the community, or the broader culture, a crucial mark of healthy congregations is their ability to deal creatively and positively with change. The fast pace of change in contemporary culture, with its bias toward, not against, change only makes the challenge of negotiating change all the more pressing for congregations.

VITAL WORSHIP

At the center of many discussions about change in churches today is the topic of worship. This is not surprising, for worship is at the center of congregational life. To "go to church" means, for most members of congregations, "to go to worship." In *How Do We Worship?*, Mark Chaves begins his analysis with the simple assertion, "Worship is the most central and public activity engaged in by American religious congregations" (Alban Institute, 1999, p. 1). Worship styles are one of the most significant reasons that people choose to join a given congregation. Correspondingly, they are central to the identity of most congregations.

Worship is also central on a much deeper level. Worship is the locus of what several Christian traditions identify as the nourishing center of congregation life: preaching, common prayer, and the celebration of ordinances or sacraments. Significantly, what many traditions elevate to the status of "the means of grace" or even the "marks of the church" are essentially liturgical actions. Worship is central, most significantly, for theological reasons. Worship both reflects and shapes a community's faith. It expresses a congregation's view of God and enacts a congregation's relationship with God and each other.

We can identify several specific factors that contribute to spiritually vital worship and thereby strengthen congregational life.

- Congregations, and the leaders that serve them, need a shared vision for worship that is grounded in more than personal aesthetic tastes. This vision must draw on the deep theological resources of Scripture, the Christian tradition, and the unique history of the congregation.
- Congregational worship should be integrated with the whole life of the congregation. It can serve as the "source and summit" from which all the practices of the Christian life flow. Worship both reflects and shapes the life of the church in education, pastoral care, community service, fellowship, justice, hospitality, and every other aspect of church life.
- The best worship practices feature not only good worship "content," such as discerning sermons, honest prayers, creative artistic contributions, celebrative and meaningful rituals for baptism and the Lord's Supper. They also arise of out of good process, involving meaningful contributions from participants, thoughtful leadership, honest evaluation, and healthy communication among leaders.

VITAL WORSHIP, HEALTHY CONGREGATIONS SERIES

The Vital Worship, Healthy Congregations Series is designed to reflect the kind of vibrant, creative energy and patient reflection that will promote worship that is both relevant and profound. It is designed to invite congregations to rediscover a common vision for worship, to sense how worship is related to all aspects of congregational life, and to imagine better ways of preparing both better "content" and better "process" related to the worship life of their own congregations.

It is important to note that strengthening congregational life through worship renewal is a delicate and challenging task precisely because of the uniqueness of each congregation. This book series is not designed to represent a single denomination, Christian tradition, or type of congregation. Nor is it designed to serve as arbiter of theological disputes about worship. Books in the series will note the significance of theological claims about worship, but they may, in fact, represent quite different theological visions from each other, or from our work at the Calvin Institute of Christian Worship. That is, the series is designed to call attention to instructive examples of congregational life and to explore these examples in ways that allow readers in very different communities to compare and contrast these examples with their own practice. The models described in any given book may for some readers be instructive as examples to follow. For others, a given example may remind them of something they are already doing well, or something they will choose not to follow because of theological commitments or community history.

In the first volume in our series, *One Bread, One Body: Exploring Cultural Diversity in Worship*, Michael Hawn posed the poignant question "is there room for my neighbor at the table?" and explored what four multicultural congregations have to teach us about hospitality and the virtues of cross-cultural worship. His work helps us step back and reflect on the core identity of our congregations.

In our second volume, *Designing Worship Together: Models and Strategies for Worship Planning*, Norma deWaal Malefyt and Howard Vanderwell enter the trenches of weekly congregational life. They give us helpful insights into the process of how services are planned and led. It is hard to overstate the significance of this topic. For without a thoughtful, discerning, collaborative worship planning process, all manner of worship books, conferences, and renewal programs are likely either to make no inroads into the life of a given congregation or, when they do, to damage rather than renew congregational life.

In the third volume, *When God Speaks through Change: Preaching in Times of Congregational Transition*, Craig Satterlee addresses the question of how worship (and particularly preaching) might best respond to times of significant congregational transition. The vast majority of published perspectives and resources for preaching and worship unwittingly assume a level of constancy in congregational life, taking for granted that the congregation will have the resources (emotional and otherwise) to absorb some significant new message or practice. However, on any given Sunday, a strikingly large number of churches are simply trying to cope with a significant transition in community life or leadership. These transitions do limit what preachers and worship leaders can do on Sunday, but they also present unparalleled opportunities for the reception of the gospel. For congregations in transition, this book provides a useful and necessary frame for viewing almost all other advice and resources about what should happen in public worship.

In this fourth volume, *Where 20 or 30 Are Gathered: Leading Worship in the Small Church,* Peter Bush and Christine O'Reilly probe a topic that is instructive not only for small congregations, but also for large ones. When representatives of small congregations attend worship conferences or read books about worship they are frequently confronted with practices and resources that are entirely impractical for their purposes, requiring time and money that simply aren't available. Yet, as Bush and O'Reilly demonstrate, "small" certainly does not mean "deficient." In fact, smaller congregations have the potential to achieve participation, flexibility, and intimacy that larger congregations find much harder to achieve. In the upside-down world of the kingdom of God, could it be that those of us from larger congregations should be attending conferences in smaller congregations, rather than just the other way around? May this volume be instructive for readers from congregations of all sizes as a stimulus to new reflection on how public worship is planned, led, and evaluated.

By promoting encounters with instructive examples from various parts of the body of Christ, we pray that these volumes will help leaders make good judgments about worship in their congregations and that, by the power of God's Spirit, these congregations will flourish.

John D. Witvliet
Calvin Institute of Christian Worship

FOREWORD

Small churches—beset by financial stress, societal disinterest, internal weariness, and unproductive patterns—have tended to hunker down and wistfully hope for a miracle. But there is another way. They can claim their identity, exert their power, and love their way toward the Kingdom. In the pages that follow, Christine O'Reilly and Peter Bush challenge small churches to put worship of God in the center of their life together and to organize that worship out of the gifts that God has already put within their congregation. This is a powerful and affirming word for small churches, which, if taken seriously, could revolutionize congregational life.

I would like to explore some of the underpinnings and implications of their approach. One is that every congregation could develop uniquely and become distinctly what God intends for them. Once churches start to organize around the Holy Spirit's gifting, the Creative God is out of the bottle! Suppose that the gift array of a particular congregation does not include a preacher or a musician or a liturgist or whatever. Yes, they could compensate for that "lack," and Bush and O'Reilly offer ways to do that. But what if what the congregation is experiencing is not a "lack" at all? Maybe God is seeking to be incarnated in some fresh way. Maybe the entire congregation could preach the sermon along the lines of the "African" Bible study model, for example. Or instead of music, the congregation could physically act out the text in differing ways each Sunday, a kind of dance of the day? OK, so I've gone over the edge. It's just that I am not seeing a lot of room for God before we reach the edge in most of our churches.

A second implication of O'Reilly and Bush's thinking is that our current practice of ordaining overeducated (but underequipped) professionals and attempting to deploy at least one of these professionals in every congregation could be given the funeral this practice so richly deserves. What's wrong with this model? Just about everything. First, it is not biblical. When I read the New Testament, I see a wide variety of Spirit-gifted people authorized to minister according to their gifts. The body of Christ is to be a body that functions interdependently, which suggests that faithful churches stop ordaining can-do-it-alls and start giving place to the calling of the many.

Second, our current model of providing professional leaders for congregations is not functional. Too much responsibility is put on one part, and the rest of the body atrophies. Many of the small churches I work with get stuck in debilitating power struggles. Of course, this is "natural," but I wonder—if people were really using their particular gifts, would they need to act out in what is perhaps a cry for importance?

Finally, the way we identify leaders for congregations is not local. Currently, people from mid-sized and large suburban churches feel the call to ordained ministry and are placed, eventually, in rural or small churches, where they act like a fish out of water because—surprise— they are! So, in many places, the arrangement is just plain not working. Maybe local people could better discern and shape ministry to the community—if local folk knew their Holy Spirit giftedness and lived it out.

A third implication of the work Bush and O'Reilly have done has to do with seminaries. Just what good are they? I personally think that they are of some use, but not the use we keep trying to put them to: equipping people to serve as pastors in congregations. In my opinion, seminaries excel at two things. Number one is helping people deepen their faith by wrestling with their often shallow understandings of an inherited faith. And second, they provide students with the tools needed to do meta-theology. Theology is applying the dynamic, relational truths of our faith to the decisions and stances of daily life. Meta-theology is the development of conceptual systems about those truths. Both are necessary to the whole enterprise of the gospel. But being a theologian, rather than a *meta*-theologian, is all that is necessary to good small (actually all) church pastoring. Tex Sample once said that seminaries make graduates "unfit to pastor real people." In the sense that pastors primarily need to communicate a vibrant, inviting theology, one that will help their flock live life aright, he is on target. Meta-theology is needed only in a small, guardian-type role. Consequently, a primary strength of seminaries is one that is not required for raising up effective pastoral ministers.

Additionally, small churches need tribal leaders, and this kind of leadership can but be pointed to in the seminary classroom. It can only be fully developed in on-the-job ministry. Some rare folk can teach themselves such leadership skills, but most of us need guides to help us learn them.

So, if these arguments are valid, do you see where this leaves us? It leaves us with this: O'Reilly and Bush have provided us a manifesto for the development of Spirit-gifted, in-culture, practical, *and*, by the way, affordable leadership for small churches.

A fourth implication has to do with a new, or I should say refound, spiritual practice. Small churches have long practiced a spirituality that was applied, relational, and life changing. This is our heritage. But, of late, spiritual practice with such qualities seems to be more a distant memory than a dynamic force. If, as this book claims, worship must be at the very core of what we do as small churches, then certain spiritual dominoes fall. We can't gaze on God's glory and be unchanged ourselves. To give glory to God is to change—to become a member of that new humanity the apostle Paul names. For some of us, a radical life change occurs at conversion followed by incremental growth toward the fullness of Christ's character. For others, becoming a "new human" is the result of ongoing cooperation with the Spirit's purpose in our life. But such change must happen or our worship is false.

Small churches afford a special context for this transformation to become effective because they can (not all do, unfortunately) provide at the same time both a safe and a challenging place for members to grow. Small churches are fundamentally relational. They function like a family. Members are accepted, loved, tolerated—the way our children, parents, siblings, aunts and uncles, cousins are. This makes the small church a very safe place, but such a protected environment does not automatically push folk to grow and mature. Other small churches are challenging, but often in a way that only the "elect" can achieve. Some small churches are safe and some are challenging, but some are both simultaneously. They have learned to build on familial acceptance and have added discipleship formation. Rather than basing their ministry on tradition, inertia, or habit, they foster a mutual commitment to growth. Members of healthy small churches already love and accept one another and so provide an ideal base upon which to add spiritual challenge.

Peter Bush and Christine O'Reilly have raised many important questions—and an earth-shattering hope—for small congregations. What if small churches worshipped God "in spirit and in truth"? What if small churches organized themselves around the spiritual giftedness of the membership? What if small churches honored multiple ministry roles, each contributing uniquely to the health of Christ's body? What if each small church became Itself, that is, became all that God intends it to be? What if small churches built traditions for developing the maturity and the ministry of each member? What if small churches perfected the art of mentoring? What if members of small churches learned to function at a high level as a team? Wow! Then even the most cynical skeptic would have to admit: there is a God!

Tony Pappas

PREFACE

"Are you *still* there?" This question, accompanied by quizzical looks, comes from clergy colleagues on a regular basis. "There" refers to the small congregations we serve, "still" to the number of years we have remained in those small congregations. These places of ministry have been challenging and rewarding, and have provided the catalyst for the content of this book. Small-membership churches are churches that focus on worship, and we passionately believe (1) that small churches can worship God with excellence, and (2) that small churches are renewed through worship. The small church survives and even thrives despite the cultural affection for "bigger is better." Clergy in particular and laity in general need encouragement and guidance in effective worship leadership in the small church. We offer this book with the humble hope that those who lead and those who worship in small congregations will find some of that encouragement and guidance within its pages.

Believing that ministry is best done in partnership, we have been enriched by many partners in this project. The congregations of Knox Presbyterian Church, Mitchell, Ontario; Knox Presbyterian Church, Thedford, Ontario; and St. Andrew's Presbyterian Church, Watford, Ontario; and the lay worship leaders of those churches have been faithful partners, giving us time to write and to teach. These churches have been our primary place of learning. The Calvin Institute of Christian Worship, Grand Rapids, Michigan, welcomed our proposals for training laypeople to plan and lead worship and for teaching the art of preaching to lay leaders. The Lilly Endowment grants received through the Institute made it possible for us to expand our commitment to lay-led worship in small congregations beyond our own locations, and to enrich congregations in southwestern Ontario; Cape Breton, Nova Scotia; northern Ontario; and western Manitoba. In each and every place, we grew in our own understanding of worship in small churches, and we were encouraged by the many gifted lay leaders who accepted the call of God to worship ministry. The enthusiastic support of John Witvliet, Cindy Holtrop, and Betty Grit was foundational not only for the worship training programs but also for this book. John's patience and perseverance in the early stages of proposals and outlines are deeply appreciated.

The work of the Alban Institute has been an asset to us in ministry and now in the process of writing this text. Beth Ann Gaede has been a delightful and diligent editor with whom to work. Her suggestions and questions not only strengthened the content of the book but also clarified our thoughts and improved our writing skills. Jean Caffey Lyles's copyediting has further improved the text and made it more accessible to readers. We are honored to have Tony Pappas write the foreword, as his writing has been formative in our ministries.

We were advised to invite a group of trusted colleagues (lay and ordained) to be the initial readers of each chapter. Their encouragement and insights proved to be invaluable. Our thanks to the Rev. Rachael Walker, the Rev. Lynn Nichol, Dr. David Ruesink, and Dr. George Bush. Since the summer of 1996, we have met monthly with other rural clergy for study, worship, and mutual encouragement. While the members of the Rural Ministry Study Group have changed over the years, the support, influence, and learning continues. Thank you to Debbie Bush, Amanda Birchall, Gloria Langois, and Johan Olivier for journeying with us through this project.

Our most important partnerships are those closest to home: our families. To Debbie and Nathan, Jesse and Clare, thank you for understanding, patience, and encouragement throughout the writing process, and for giving us the freedom to travel and wonderful reasons to come home.

> Young men and women alike, old and young together!
> Let them praise the name of the Lord,
> For his name alone is exalted;
> His glory is above earth and heaven.
>
> Psalm 148:12-13

O come, let us worship God!

CHAPTER 1

BLEST BE THE TIE THAT BINDS

Models of Congregational Ministry

It was Monday morning. Debra Howard sat at her desk and looked out the window. Recently returned from a worship conference, she was wrestling with the many ideas that had sounded so wonderful, and with the reality that had confronted her yesterday as she led worship at River Valley Church. Twenty-two worshipers had faced her from the old oak pews in the small sanctuary. Twenty-two, including Mrs. Benson on the piano and the three souls who made up the choir. "How on earth," Debra wondered aloud, "can we ever hope to have worship like it was at the conference? They had PowerPoint litanies, a contemporary praise team, liturgical dance, and a dramatic presentation of the Scripture text. We can't even agree on new hymnbooks, let alone afford to buy them!"

Easing onto the highway for the morning commute to his office at TJR Engineering, Joel Brennan thought back to yesterday morning's worship service at Gordon Memorial Church. Thirty-six voices had sung the hymns that faintly echoed in a sanctuary designed for 150. The style of the service had reflected the 150 rather than the 36, with a vast distance between preacher and people. The distance was as much spiritual as physical. An atmosphere of discouragement blended with dogged determination among the gathered community of faith. Joel asked himself what lay ahead for Gordon Memorial. "I believe God is with us, and wants to do something at our church. I wonder if renewing our worship services is a place to begin?"

Perhaps you, a pastor or member of a small church, can see yourself in Debra or Joel. While worship is the primary purpose of all churches, worship in the small church is distinctive. Whether in a house church, a newly organized church, a rural church along a country road, or a city church whose neighborhood demographics have shifted, worship with fewer than 40 people is simply different from worship with 75. These small faith communities present unique opportunities and challenges for worship leaders.

This chapter seeks to lay out some of the features common to small churches whatever their geographic location or place in the congregational life cycle. No two small congregations are the same, although there are common keys to understanding and approaching ministry in various contexts. The idiosyncratic nature of a given small congregation is governed by its history, its community and cultural context, and the personalities of its leaders. History and tradition matter, whether measured in centuries or years. Traditions around events like the first Sunday of Advent or the congregation's anniversary are foundational in congregational self-definition, even if the numbers of events and programs in small congregations are few.

The community in which a church stands helps form congregational identity. Sometimes the congregation reflects the community; sometimes it finds its identity by differentiating itself from the community. For example, a church in a mining town includes among its members both company executives and those who mine the ore. On the other hand, a congregation in a city suburb struggles to maintain a Scots-Irish identity as waves of immigration change the ethnic makeup of the neighborhood. People may drive great distances to attend a particular small church, doing so because of a connection to the church in that place, either through family ties or through a sense of call to the ministry of the congregation. Small churches in the same community, representing a variety of denominations, may share more in common across denominational lines than they share with small churches of their own denomination in another community. Differences in polity or doctrine may be set aside to maintain cultural connection and cooperation, especially for ethnic congregations emerging in North American cities, where linguistic and cultural connections are valued more highly than denominationalism.

It is crucial that clergy and congregational leaders who come from outside the congregational culture spend time learning the unique culture of the small church they serve. Without such an understanding, worship and mission will not be appropriate to the context. Discernment of the congregation's sense of itself and of the community it serves will enable clergy to minister effectively in all areas of church life, including meaningful worship. The task of educated reflection on the congregation is equally important for its lay leaders. These faithful people may have been part of the church for many years, but may not have given sustained thought to either the congregational culture or the culture of the wider community. If worship is to be authentic to its cultural context, it must be led by leaders who understand the culture.

THE NATURE OF THE SMALL CHURCH

In the literature discussing church size, congregations of fewer than 50 are described as "family size" churches.[1] These congregations generally behave like a family unit with a patriarch/matriarch/oligarch who functions as "permission giver" or "gatekeeper." Names and personal histories of members are often common knowledge. Within these congregations an atmosphere of belonging, acceptance, genuine concern, and loyalty prevails. Absences are noted, people are missed, and phone calls or visits express a deep caring. Church family ties are strong. The nine-year-old beginning violinist is invited to play the offertory, and the congregation beams, oblivious to a missed note. The 75-year-old woman whose voice is not as strong and whose eyesight is not as clear as it used to be still leads the Responsive Psalm. Members of small churches "have learned to hang together as a congregation, learning to live together with difficult brothers and sisters in the faith, and learning to worship the Triune God in a style that is not quite theirs."[2]

Small congregations are built upon intimacy and relationships that have taken years—generations, in fact—to develop. Nearly all of us come from other places to ministry in small churches. It is natural for clergy to view the congregations they serve as "other," as "they" or "them," rather than as "we" and "us." Lay leaders within the congregation may share that view. Clergy need to invest in relationships, which will in turn require both self and time. Pastors need to "join the church," identifying themselves with the people they serve.

The move from "they" to "we" is illustrated powerfully in the story of Father Joseph Damien deVeuster (1840-1889), a priest who volunteered, much to the dismay of his superiors, to serve a colony of lepers on the Hawaiian island of Molokai. Father Damien threw himself into the work, organizing construction projects, but he kept an emotional and physical distance from his flock. After some time, Damien realized that truly to minister to the colony, he needed to bridge that gap. He began thinking in Pauline terms and wrote, "I make myself a leper with the lepers to gain all to Jesus Christ. That is why, in preaching, I say 'we lepers.'" Damien would realize the full impact of these words when, in 1884, he accidentally spilled some boiling water on his foot—and instead of the pain he expected, felt nothing. This absence of feeling was an unmistakable sign that the disease which was "theirs" had now become "his." The story of Damien's passionate ministry and concern for his flock is held in high honor to this day.[3]

Effective ministry in small churches requires this depth of dedication to and identification with "the flock." Pastors in small congregations need to think, speak, and act with a "we" attitude and conviction. It is crucial for pastors to recognize that

- this ministry and these people are important;
- this congregation deserves a ministry of excellence;
- God is present and at work in and through this congregation;
- an important ministry role is serving as an advocate for small membership churches.

A caveat: one of the challenges clergy face is to develop this depth of identification and commitment and yet be differentiated enough to grasp the larger vision for that congregation and the concerted effort needed to pursue the vision. In the article "Learning to Pastor a Small Congregation," which he wrote while serving as pastor of Good Shepherd Lutheran Church on the West Side of Chicago, Andrew Hagen offers this metaphor and comment:

> If this church were a ship, my role as pastor was not to have a hand on
> the tiller steering its course but rather a seat in the crow's nest looking

for dangers and opportunities ahead. Since pastoral turnover in smaller churches is relatively frequent, the congregation is legitimately concerned about pastors who set the course and then abandon ship. But they truly value the education and vision of their pastors and rely upon them to prevent them from looking only to the past.[4]

As clergy learn to find their place in the small church, gatherings of small-church leaders, opportunities for education, and exposure to the practices of worship and ministry in a variety of places are an enriching and broadening experience. The Calvin Institute of Christian Worship offered such an opportunity during a worship renewal grants colloquium in June 2004. In a group discussion about small churches, the gifts and challenges listed in the accompanying boxes were identified.

Gifts of Small Congregations

- Intimacy
- Rapid communication
- History
- Personal identity
- Trust in God
- Hope
- Versatility
- Hospitality
- Rapid response to needs
- Flexibility in worship

Challenges of Small Congregations

- Perceived self-limits
- Expectations of what should be
- Burnout
- Focus on survival, not mission
- Competition with other congregations
- History that binds
- Lack of resources (people and finances)
- Rapidly changing world
- Fear of risk-taking

THE ROLE OF CLERGY

Small-membership congregations tend to experience high clergy turn-over. The reasons are many. In their excellent work *Discovering Hope*, Lutheran theologians and small-church specialists David Poling-Goldenne and L. Shannon Jung write:

> Limited size, financial constraints, congregational history and nega-
> tive self-image can cause pastors and members to feel hopeless and
> ineffective. In fact, in a survey of pastors . . . negative self-image was
> shown to be the number one problem facing the smaller churches by a
> 2-to-1 margin. Negative self-image is the silent killer of many churches
> today. Tired of trying, worn out by limited thinking, and burdened by
> economic realities, many congregations become complacent, turn in
> upon themselves, and give up—sometimes without fully realizing they
> are doing this.[5]

These same factors affect clergy and result in a desire to move to "greener pastures," usually a larger, more affluent congregation. Congregations with a negative self-image may not only accept this trend, but approve of it: "We can't hold Pastor James back." Small congregations live in the shadow of the large church and in a society where success is measured numerically. "Bigger is better" is the byword of the age. The more people in worship, the more children in Sunday school, the more financial resources in the bank, the better the church is. This attitude often leads to evaluation practices that can chronically erode the self-esteem of small congregations whose numbers are reported in single or double digits, and leave their leaders constantly disheartened.

Clergy are not immune to the "bigger is better" mantra. Direct or indirect pressure from colleagues, denominational officials, family, and self can leave pastors wondering about their personal worth and professional effectiveness. They often feel "stuck" in a location, fear that their talents are being wasted, or struggle with great disappointment about the gap between their vision and the reality with which they must deal. These attitudes will, at least subtly, permeate everything. Wise ministers will seek out and take advantage of resources that highlight and increase understanding of the nature and fabric of the small church, with its richness and complexity. Such resources will strengthen both clergy and their congregations.

The high turnover of clergy in small congregations affects the ways those churches relate to a new minister. The description "chaplain" is sometimes used in this context. Ministers are valued as providers of traditional pastoral care and good preaching, with a "steady hand on the tiller." New ideas and programs introduced by the minister are generally viewed with caution or reluctance, since the next pastor may go a different direction. Since relationships are of primary importance in the small-membership church, an atmosphere of trust between clergy and congregation is crucial for all decision making. Trust is earned slowly, often only by consistent ministry over a period of years, even a decade. Clergy prepared to be adopted into the family and to embrace a long-term pastorate will find such ministry rewarding, since the relationship of trust establishes a foundation and a reason for a congregation to consider, accept, and implement change. This long tenure, in turn, may lead to congregational growth in both population and spiritual maturity. A key foundation for such growth can be congregational worship. Worship leadership that is inclusive, personal, and contextually based strengthens a congregation and broadens its vision so that the members embrace God's call to ministry and mission.

Decision making in the "family church" usually happens by consensus. Outwardly, boards, committees, and management will follow church polity; inwardly, church leaders may still defer to the unwritten but clearly understood system of approval. Time must be given for consultation and discussion prior to any formal decision. Change in this context is possible, if those leading or advocating the change work with an understanding of the system, and with the virtues of humility, patience, courage, and respect. Worship practices and traditions can be held very deeply in this context, with particularities unique to each congregation. The renewal of worship practices, and any changes to worship traditions, must therefore be decided corporately and carefully.

WORSHIP IN THE SMALL CHURCH

Worship is the most important and most consistent element of congregational life. It is the practice of worship that defines a church as a church, and not a social club or service organization. The size of a church has a direct impact on worship. While some believe that small congregations cannot meet the needs of current and future generations with sufficient "programming options," we contend that programs are secondary to faithful, effective congregational ministry. Although small faith communities cannot pack the church building 24/7 with small groups, classes, music rehearsals, and the like, they can provide vibrant worship that honors God and reminds worshipers of their identity and calling in Jesus Christ. God is present with and empowers the faithful in worship, as the scriptures testify: "But You are holy, O You who dwell in the praises of Israel" (Ps. 22:3 AMP).

Vibrant worship undergirds church life beyond weekly gatherings, providing a strong sense of community and deeply personal pastoral care. It is our belief that small congregations can remind the wider church that the very purpose of any church, regardless of size, is to be a people who worship God.

Small congregations take on many forms. They may be single-point, solo-pastor ministries; yoked congregations served by the same minister; or congregations "clustered" with a ministry team. Congregations may receive full or partial denominational financial assistance, and congregations in any of these configurations may be led entirely by laypeople or clergy, either full- or part-time. The form of organization is often defined by economics rather than by mission or ministry needs and can itself influence how the congregation functions. Judicatory bodies also play a role in these settings. Such factors affect congregational self-esteem, leadership style, and autonomy.

Most clergy in small churches come from urban or suburban backgrounds and are recent seminary graduates, steeped in city and university life. Small congregations—particularly those in rural or remote communities, with their strong traditions, unwritten codes of conduct, and weariness at "breaking in" another pastor—can leave clergy in a state of culture shock, learning to speak a new language and to navigate a new life. Clergy may find themselves echoing the psalmist's lament: "How can we sing the songs of the Lord while in a foreign land?" (Ps. 137:4 NIV). In preparing for worship, clergy probably face an indigenous liturgy that may bear little or no resemblance to the careful teachings of seminary professors, while members assume that the way they worship is the pattern used by *all* congregations.

Worshipers may be familiar with a small, select repertoire of music. The hymnals in use may be from another time or tradition. Prayer books and other worship guides may not be the most recent editions promoted by the denomination. Practices around communion, baptism, prayer, and seasonal celebrations are steeped in the traditions of that particular congregation. Weddings and funerals bring another set of expectations. Clergy must learn the ways of worship in *this* congregation, and honor those practices as they seek to renew worship.

> *St. John's Church celebrated communion only four times each year. Each communion was imbued with a sense of discomfort, much to the disappointment of the minister, Lois McDermott. Lois noticed that the communion cup holders, where worshipers placed empty individual cups after drinking the grape juice, were available only in the pews on the north side of the sanctuary. When she asked one of the longtime members about this oddity, this story was told: in former years, communion services marked a sharp division within the congregation—only official members in good standing were allowed to participate, a practice reinforced as the congregation was formally separated into "member" and "nonmember" pews. Families were split, with husbands and wives, parents and children sitting on opposite sides of the church. Lois approached the elders about communion practices and invited conversation about the Lord's Supper at St. John's. Gradually, and with the foundation laid in sermons and Bible studies on worship in general and communion in particular, St. John's began celebrating the sacrament with a sense of grace and joy. There were murmurs of delight when additional communion cup holders were installed so that they were available in every pew, and the congregation enjoyed the Lord's Supper as a united family.*

> *Helene duPlanchet had grown up in a small church in Nova Scotia's Acadian region. She accepted a call to become pastor at Peace Church in Western Canada. Her first opportunity to officiate at a funeral took place a few weeks after Helene arrived at Peace. She led the service with dignity and compassion, at both the funeral home and the cemetery. She then returned to her study at the manse, and resumed preparation for Sunday's service. Later that night, Helene received a phone call from Wilma Kreider, president of the Ladies Aid. The family of the deceased had been deeply upset, and*

the Ladies Aid members deeply embarrassed that Helene did not come to the church for the funeral lunch. Helene was hurt and irritated—she did not know that this, too, was part of her pastoral role. In her home community, funeral lunches were attended only by family members.

At the same time clergy are learning the customs of the small church, they must discover their place as worship planners and leaders. With a small number of people to work with, clergy are often tempted to take on too many responsibilities and roles in worship. They plan and lead every aspect of the service alone, from reading Scripture to selecting hymns. Some musically gifted clergy may even accompany the singing to the exclusion of other instrumentalists. Production of the weekly order of service and announcements may be theirs, too—accompanied by complaints that they receive little or no help from the congregation. Preparation for ministry and personal gratification may contribute to this pattern. As students, clergy are often taught in, and thus emulate, a "lone ranger" style, as opposed to a more collegial approach to ministry. Clergy and church members alike may accept the tradition that "the minister" is "the expert" in worship and the professional at the task of worship leadership. Members who have endured yet another period without a pastor gladly breathe a sigh of relief, grateful that someone else can now assume the tasks they have borne for so long. However, the wisest course for the long-term health of both minister and church is to work as a team, partners in worship preparation and leadership. Scripture teaches that all of God's people have gifts to be used in the work of the ministry (see Eph. 4:11-13). Clergy self-care demands that the tasks of ministry be shared. A servant-leader model of ministry avoids the potential of a "worship expert" being elevated above the worshipers.

Small congregations, like all churches, look for excellence in worship leaders. In the search for a new minister, they long for a skilled leader who will value the understanding and traditions of their faith community. Laity may feel fatigued after a time without a called minister, either having assumed many responsibilities themselves, or having endured a new worship leader each week. When a new minister arrives, a mixture of curiosity and cautious optimism abounds. People hope the relationship with this pastor will be a good and long one; yet they wonder if this minister will stay long enough to be trusted. If the relationship between the congregation and the minister proves to be difficult, the question becomes, "How much longer will he be here?" If the relationship with the minister becomes one of respect, trust, and deep affection, and if the minister is perceived as skilled and gifted, the question takes on another nuance: "How much longer will she be here? She is too good to stay in a small church like ours for very long." Questions about "how long the minister will stay" form an undercurrent in the congregation, even as members brace themselves for the usual round of changes and new ideas that doubtless will surface.

Clergy serving small churches would be wise to keep in mind that those who are part of a small church have a deep commitment to their congregation and to its worship life. While these faith communities may appear resistant to change, they are in fact very much aware of the benefits and pitfalls of change. The need for change is recognized; how and why change happens are critical factors both clergy and laity must consider as they seek worship renewal. Articulated or not, a theology of worship resides deep in the ethos of the congregation. People have their own beliefs and understanding of worship and how worship "ought to be." Discovering and developing a working theology of worship in a faith community is a task for both pastor and people. From this foundation, solid worship renewal is possible and even desired by those in the pulpit and the pew, provided that such renewal is undertaken after an atmosphere of trust has been achieved and that the process is accompanied by careful teaching and respectful listening.

WORSHIP IN MULTI-POINT OR YOKED CONGREGATION

Many of the characteristics of small churches discussed above are equally applicable to single-point and multi-point pastoral charges. However, multi-point and yoked congregations must deal with some unique issues regarding worship.

Pastors of multi-point charges are rather like parents of multiple children. Each congregation has its own personality, history, building, traditions, needs, and strengths. Learning, understanding, and respect are essential for effective ministry and worship leadership. The pastor must be perceived as treating each congregation fairly and equitably. Worship practices and congregational events need not be the same in two or more yoked congregations, but it is essential that each church feel valued, cared for, and ministered to. Clergy who know the unique traits of each congregation they serve, and who build upon those traits as they plan and lead worship, will find that the effort bears fruit. Worship services in this setting will not necessarily be identical in each congregation, but each will require equity of effort and attitude on the part of the pastor.

Types of Yoked or Multi-point Congregations

An endless variety of configurations is possible in yoked or multi-point ministry churches:

- Traditional two- or three-point charge served by a minister.
- Congregations from different denominations sharing one minister.
- Cluster or cooperating ministry: a group of congregations works together in a "team ministry" approach for all aspects of church life. The "ministry team" is designed by and made up of a variety of people with a variety of gifts, accountable to *all* congregations in the cluster.

Hope Church is a congregation with loyal family ties. Members are cautious with finances and have developed an inner strength from a succession of short-term pastorates. A century of worshiping in the same neo-Gothic building has given them many memories to cherish and traditions to uphold. The people of Hope Church have faced the demographic shifts common to most rural communities, but their worship attendance is a stable 46, including several young families. They exhibit an air of self-confidence, especially as they look over at their partner church, Zion–Mount McConan.

Zion–Mount McConan, smaller than Hope, is the result of a presbytery-led amalgamation of congregations 15 kilometers apart, about nine miles. Zion had been struggling with a dozen faithful souls, and Mount McConan sheltered 15 on Sunday mornings. It just seemed to make sense that the two join together, making— along with Hope—a more attractive two-point ministry setting, rather than a burdensome three-point charge. Zion's building was farthest from Hope Church, and required more repair than Mount

McConan's. The decision was made to close Zion's building, and to put "Zion" first in the new congregation's name. Lead families from each church were determined to make the new arrangement work. Difficult as the amalgamation had been at times, the result was a community of faith open to blending new ideas with old traditions. Twenty-four dedicated people, mostly seniors, gathered Sunday by Sunday to worship.

John Elliott, a recent seminary graduate, had been the pastor of these congregations for just over a year. He had carefully followed the common wisdom, "Don't change anything for a year," and he was now eager to introduce some new music to worship services. John preferred to display the words of a hymn using an overhead projector, a change that would require a financial investment from both congregations in addition to a willingness on the part of members to try new songs. John raised the matter at Hope Church's elders meeting. After an awkward silence, concerns were noted one by one. The words of these new songs would not be as rich as traditional hymns. The music was too reminiscent of popular radio tunes. One elder was upset that worship would become a "sound and light show," losing a sense of dignity and proper reverence. All present agreed that a projection screen was not in keeping with the architecture of the sanctuary, but there was no suitable wall space to project upon, and nowhere that the choir singers (who faced the congregation) could see the words without craning their necks. John felt discouraged.

The agenda for the Zion–Mount McConan elders meeting had already been printed, so the topic was raised for discussion there the next night. Much to John's surprise, the elders were open to the idea. After discussing some practical concerns, they agreed to give the proposal a three-month trial. Archie Johnson, the retired custodian of the local school, agreed to look into borrowing an overhead projector. John drove home elated.

His elation would be short-lived, however. Mary Winton, president of the Hope Church Ladies Aid, typed the weekly bulletins shared by both congregations. She was more than dismayed to notice the change John had made in the order of service; he had added another line: a "new song" to be sung at "Zion–Mount McConan only." Worship at Zion–Mount McConan went well that Sunday.

The new song was warmly received, and people commented on it as they greeted John after the service. The last people to leave were an elderly couple who asked to speak with John for a moment. After hearing that their granddaughter was seriously ill, John offered a prayer with them, and promised to visit the next day. Since he was now running late for the service at Hope Church, he drove well above the speed limit in an effort to be there on time. Dashing from the car to the church, John was greeted by three elders with stony faces. "Late today, John? Hmmm. You know we like to start on time here. Perhaps the 'new music' at Zion makes their service too long." Don Andrews's voice had a distinct edge to it. The three turned and walked up the steps to the sanctuary, leaving John somewhere between discouragement and anger. He adjusted his robe and tried to adjust his attitude. He had to lead worship, after all.

This story captures a variety of the circumstances and issues faced by pastors and yoked congregations in worship. Time pressures, fairness (real and perceived), congregational pride, and the relationship between the points all affect their worship life, individually and together. One relatively minor change in worship practice can set everyone on a collision course. The impact is felt by pastor and parishioners, between them, and between the yoked congregations.

Here are some of our reflections on this story. What are your thoughts?

- How will this episode affect John as he prepares worship for the next Sunday?
- Some members at Hope Church were concerned for John that morning; they sensed that he was not his usual self in worship that day.
- What might happen at next month's meeting of the elders from both congregations?
- Mary Winton met Archie Johnson at the post office that week, and commented, "So—you folks have a different worship service than we do now."
- Don Andrews loved his church. He did not love change. He also valued punctuality, and he had agreed to attend his grandson's piano recital that afternoon. Don was worried that the church

service would run overtime, forcing him either to leave church early or to arrive late to the recital.

These are but a few of the spin-off concerns arising from experiences like this, which affect individuals, congregations, and pastoral charges on many levels.

Worship planning, preparation, and leadership cannot be divorced from daily life in any community or congregation. The task grows more complex when more than one community and congregation are involved.

WORSHIP IN CONGREGATIONS BETWEEN OR WITHOUT CLERGY

Greenway Church was an attractive brick building nestled in a subdivision of a major city. Built in the 1950s, it was designed to meet the needs of those settling into the suburbs, purchasing their own homes, and raising their families. The sanctuary seated 120; the floor below housed a multipurpose hall and a kitchen. Located away from the busy main streets, the church had a "neighborhood" feel to it and had been a place of worship and nurture for 40 families. Although the numbers had never reached their full potential, church life had been satisfying with Christmas concerts, a talented choir, and a variety of committees and organizations. The congregation had been led and nurtured by a couple of much-loved ministers and a small but strong group of lay leaders.

But that was then—this was now. Greenway Church had changed over the years. Children had grown up and left. The original homeowners were older. Some of them had grown frail and had moved to seniors' residences. The "neighborhood feel" changed, as people from different parts of the world, speaking different languages and observing different religious traditions, moved in. A much-loved pastor accepted a call elsewhere, to be followed by a minister who ran into difficulties with conflict. After he left, Greenway Church was truly struggling. Church finances grew tighter, the Sunday school grew smaller, and leaders grew increasingly anxious. It was decided that half-time ministry was all the congregation could afford—a decision that led to a string of short-term pastorates. Sunday morning attendance dwindled to 30, with two or three children in

Sunday school on an irregular basis. Only a few came from the Greenway neighborhood, the remaining stalwart members driving in from their seniors' apartments some distance away, weather permitting. When the last half-time minister resigned to stay at home with her young children, Greenway Church was once again declared "vacant" by the presbytery, and the session (the congregation's governing body) was directed to develop a strategic plan for its future viability. That was two years ago; Greenway Church is still "vacant," and the members are still trying to ascertain their future. Worship services are led by an assortment of retired clergy and lay speakers. The congregation longs for a sense of continuity, familiarity, and clear direction for their future.

All congregations find themselves "in between" or without called or appointed clergy from time to time. Small congregations tend to find themselves in this position with regularity, sometimes for an extended duration—a situation that affects the congregation in many ways. As Dean Hoge, professor of sociology at the Catholic University of America, and Jacqueline Wenger, a research associate at the same institution, noted in their "Pulpit & Pew" study, *Pastors in Transition: Why Clergy Leave Local Church Ministry*: "Small churches cannot find the ministers they need. For some denominations the problem may be worsening."[6]

Judicatory bodies find these congregations and their frequent (and long) vacancies frustrating. Such churches appear to require more time than the number of members warrants, increasing the workload for those with judicatory responsibility. In addition to covering pastoral-care needs, finding individuals to lead worship on a regular basis, and often for some time, is problematic. Small congregations expect and deserve excellent care and worship—ministries that may actually require more attention during times of discernment and change. While denominational polities vary, judicatories are often faced with giving the responsibility for such congregations to their most inexperienced or overworked personnel. With all these factors combined, judicatory staff may develop an unspoken attitude of "just go away"—an attitude that does not escape the attention of the members of small churches.

Regular periods without clergy leadership leave their mark on congregations. They come to distrust judicatories, whose officials may be perceived as wanting to close the congregation because it is "so small." A sense of weariness and an erosion of self-esteem become evident because yet another minister has left (often for a larger, "more rewarding" position). Congregations often develop the ability to survive—an adaptation that can reflect both strength and intransigence. The strength arises from members who assume roles that make use of and allow them to hone their gifts, a shared determination for the well-being of the congregation, and relationships that deepen with every new challenge. However, intransigence toward new ideas and ambivalence toward developing a relationship of trust with the new minister also grow. Proposals that the congregation considers a new model of ministry are often met with resistance. Having endured such proposals before (and being likely to endure them again and again), these congregations question what, if any, benefits may accrue through the upheaval of more change. Attracting clergy to these congregations grows increasingly difficult as the churches gain a reputation of being "difficult" or "contentious."

Lay leaders face additional challenges. While they are using their God-given gifts, the danger of burnout is high. These leaders may feel that they are "working two jobs," and doing so without the support of adequate preparation and ready resources. Even in congregations with the most gifted lay leaders, constraints of time and energy divert efforts away from outreach and congregational development toward the tasks of administration.

Numerous congregations on downtown streets and along country roads will not be led by a called or appointed pastor. This experience may last a decade, or it may simply be the model of church that the members accept. Clergy shortages, financial constraints, local history, denominational policy, and reluctance on the part of ministers to accept calls to these situations are all contributing factors. Yet these communities of faith still yearn for corporate worship, which is in fact their raison d'être.

ECUMENICAL MINISTRY

Through the 1970s and 1980s, communities were built in response to mining or logging opportunities, or to carry out long-term construction projects (for example, erecting hydroelectric dams). These communities, in remote parts of North America, presented denominational leaders with a dual challenge

- to minister to members of their denominations living in these communities when numbers did not warrant a resident pastor;
- to do ministry under the terms established by the companies and governments funding the projects, which controlled what was built, and insisted that only one church building be constructed.

These conditions forced ecumenical conversations. In some cases, elaborate administrative structures were developed; in other cases much more ad hoc committees worked out the details of the relationships.

There have been two kinds of responses to these inventions. The first has been to see them as unique and specific arrangements that had little application to the broader church. Leaders following this approach have insisted, for example, that members of these ecumenical congregations identify their denominational affiliation so that they can have their children baptized or dedicated and can participate in communion in the denominationally approved manner. In fact, the congregation has become a collection of smaller congregations worshiping together, with each smaller congregation maintaining its identity within the whole.

A second approach has been to create a new congregation that is truly one, sharing the strengths and blessings of all represented. Denominational policies and practices are modified and blended, with the focus of the faith community directed toward the foundations of what is common to the churches' doctrine and discipleship. So parents who were baptized in Anglican congregations, grew up Anglican, and define themselves as Anglican, celebrate the opportunity to have their children dedicated, not baptized, as an act of Christian worship and commitment.

Ecumenical cooperation is seen as an increasingly attractive option for small churches, but as the group of small-church leaders gathered by the Calvin Institute of Christian Worship noted, it will take great skill and wise leadership to develop workable models. No single approach will fit all cases, and designers will need to think through the cultural and administrative challenges creatively. For example, when Atomic Energy of Canada Ltd. was establishing its research facility at Pinawa, Manitoba, the leaders of the churches represented at the Chalk River, Ontario, plant came together with the intention of forming one ecumenical congregation in the new community. Those people who knew they were being transferred to Pinawa and were part of congregations in Chalk River formed a steering committee for the new church. The committee made up of Anglicans, Lutherans, Presbyterians, Baptists, and United Church of Canada members spent time talking, praying, listening, and planning. Out of this conversation, a model of church developed that respects and incorporates the variety of traditions represented. For example, Pinawa Christian Fellowship

- offers both infant baptism and child dedication;
- selects leaders on the basis of their gifts and spiritual discernment rather than a balance of denominational representation;
- holds worship services during Holy Week that include the stations of the cross and an informal sunrise Easter service.

This model of ministry and worship was born out of considerable time and effort. Any effective ecumenical ministry requires no less and must keep as its focus the worship of God who calls the church, whatever its form, into being.

A POSTLUDE

Worship is the heart of the church, regardless of location, size, and denomination. The characteristics of the small church shape and influence worship. The small-membership congregation's intimate relationships, decision-making style, and organizational structure all bear upon the way its people praise God. Regardless of a congregation's size, denomination, or style, the heart of worship remains consistent: in worship, God is honored. In worship the church remembers who it is, and individual members are reminded of who they are in Christ. In worship the church is renewed for its mission to the world. In worship the congregation is given the strength and resources to live in opposition to a culture that sees God as irrelevant. Worship matters. As the contemporary faith statement of the Presbyterian Church in Canada proclaims:

> The church lives to praise God.
> We have no higher calling
> than to offer the worship that belongs to God

day by day, Sunday by Sunday.
Through the preaching of the Word,
and the celebration of the Sacraments,
in praise, prayer, teaching and fellowship,
God sustains the life of the church.

From *Living Faith: A Statement of Christian Belief*, 7.3.1, 7.3.2

CHAPTER 2

JESUS, WHERE'ER THY PEOPLE MEET

The Joys and Challenges of Small-Church Worship

In the popular movie My Big Fat Greek Wedding, *Gus Portokalos is deeply distressed that his daughter Toula is marrying a "xeno"— a non-Greek man, Ian Miller. Such a thing has never happened in his family, and Gus is upset. Only at the wedding reception do we discover that Gus has finally come to terms with his daughter's choice. Indulging his favorite pastime of etymology, Gus finds Greek origins in every word—including the surname "Miller." Miller, he tells the guests, comes from the Greek word* mila, *which means "apple."* Portokalos *comes from the Greek word meaning "orange."*

"So," Gus concludes, "what we have here are apples and oranges.... But, in the end, we're all fruit." The couple and the crowd express their approval in laughter and applause—with hugs for both the bride and the groom.

As we explore the joys and challenges of worship in the small church, readers may find some descriptions that mesh with their own experience, along with others that do not. Small churches come as "apples and oranges" too, with unique personalities and histories, but they share a common faith and a desire to worship God. In that respect, small churches are "all fruit," to borrow from Gus Portokalos' imagery; small churches are all places where the faithful and the seeking gather for worship. Whatever form or tradition the worship follows, "the major focus," say theologians and ecclesiologists William Willimon and Robert Wilson, "will be on the thing the church of small membership does best: it provides a Christian community where the people participate in worship, hear the Word, and carry on a ministry to one another and to the larger community."[1]

It is easy for members, ministers, denominational leaders, and those who work in ecclesiastical think tanks to focus on the problems facing the small congregation. To be sure, these problems require honest evaluation. There are also tremendous joys and strengths within the small church, and these, too, require honest evaluation and appreciation. We have observed that the greatest joys of small-membership churches may also be among their greatest challenges.

THE CHALLENGES

As with all types of ministry, small-church ministry offers challenges to those in either pew or pulpit. Recognition of the specific challenges, the limitations, and the opportunities they provide, assists leaders in their effectiveness with these faith communities.

Limited Resources

An obvious challenge faced by small-membership congregations is the size of the resource base. Simply put, fewer resources are at hand. The number of people involved puts limits on both the financial support and the human skills available. Small churches that are already stretched to pay a minister and to keep the building standing may long for the money to purchase new choir music and PowerPoint technology, and long just as fervently for the personnel to lead a music program and to operate new equipment. Members of small churches may fold their arms and declare, "We don't need that stuff anyway," or may wring their hands and lament, "We're so small we can't do much."

Resistance to anything that might cost money can become a pattern of resisting all change. Members often believe that the limited finances available are to be stored up for a "rainy day," rather than invested to advance the mission. In addition, people can become overextended, as they volunteer for yet one more task, or they may feel "out of their depth" when asked to serve in areas beyond their skills and gifts. All these responses can lead a congregation away from its purpose of glorifying God.

Music in worship plays an important role. In one congregation, a rotation of pianists was set up after the full-time organist moved. Susie felt that she should volunteer, even though she couldn't play well. After all, there were so few pianists available. But the month Susie took her turn, the music dragged and was played badly. People began avoiding church when Susie was the pianist. In another church, a member taught himself to play the organ in case he was needed to "fill in." Although he was capable of playing the hymns, Arthur's ability did not lend itself to leading choral music. When Arthur acted as substitute organist, no choir anthems were offered, much to the disappointment of the congregation.

Tanya Johnson and Tyler Smithfield attended a synod-wide youth event and thoroughly enjoyed the style of worship and the songbooks that were used. Upon returning, they wrote a letter to the elders at Creekside Church, asking that copies of the songbook be purchased for their own services. Twenty books would serve this small church well. But the request was rejected, with the explanation, "Money is tight right now." Tanya and Tyler were discouraged and began driving into the city to attend a contemporary service at a large new church.

The annual congregational meeting reached the point everyone dreaded: nominations for committees and responsibilities. The Rev. Doreen Lawlor looked over the list and then looked out over the 15 souls who huddled together on the wooden chairs in the church basement. Faithful but tired of carrying all the commitments, the same people found their names slotted into the same positions for yet another year. Doreen sighed inwardly, knowing that the Sunday school would struggle again under Martha McCusker's well-intentioned but outdated style as superintendent. But who else was there?

When leaders and members focus almost exclusively on the shortage of resources, then discouragement, fatigue, and a sense of entrapment can haunt a small church. Such an obsession reduces the desire both to worship with enthusiasm and to minister with vision. We believe that this obsession leads to the small church's becoming even smaller, as self-preservation and survival replace vitality and a heart for mission.

The Limits of Buildings

The church building itself can pose enormous challenges. Steep stairs, unyielding pews, and somber surroundings in a cavernous sanctuary can make worship an intimidating experience. Such an environment can impede the intimacy so crucial to the life of any small congregation. Windows, plaques, and memorabilia, as well as the architecture itself, may render walls unsuitable for hanging banners or using a projector. The placement of pulpits, lecterns, and the sacramental furniture of font and table can be an impediment to a contemporary style of worship. Even such mundane issues as the availability of electrical outlets can present problems. Changing or altering these items can prove structurally difficult, architecturally incongruent, expensive, and hurtful to those who have contributed to the sacred items every church possesses.

A growing congregation with a building over a century old struggles to maintain the integrity of the architecture while seeking ways to provide accessibility for the elderly and physically challenged. There are 10 steps from the street up to the sanctuary, and the only washroom facilities are located in the basement, which can be reached only by navigating down a spiral staircase or by going back outside the building and maneuvering down another flight of steps.

Eager to use new music projected via an overhead, St. Aidan's Chapel faced two problems: a "screen" of stucco walls that distorted the words, and a choir loft placed so that the singers would have to look back over their shoulders to see the projected lyrics.

While these matters are not unique to the small church, congregations where 20 or 30 gather may not have access to the financial resources or to the hours of hands-on labor equal to the enormous task of building renovations, restorations, and replacements.

Limited Relationships

While there is comfort in being part of a family in a small congregation, it is equally true that families face internal conflicts. Anonymity offers a security that does not exist in the small church. Family feuds, children in trouble with the law, financial problems, and personal opinions are often public knowledge. "Open secrets" may abound in small churches, where everyone knows someone's personal business but no one says anything, at least not to those directly involved. Because of the ultimate importance of relationships within the family and the ultimate quest to keep the church family together, anything that might provoke hurt feelings or outright conflict is avoided. Therefore, some people are not considered for certain roles ("We can't ask *them* to do *that!*"), while others are deluged with too many roles or placed in roles for which they are unsuited ("But Joyce has *always* been in charge!"). Others may take personal possession of a particular task, excluding others intentionally or unintentionally.

Faced with the challenges that result from the politics of relationships, members sometimes take comfort in the knowledge that "We've always done it this way." Unfortunately, this mind-set can stifle change and opportunity; it stunts both honest reflection and constructive criticism.

Reid Davis, one of three elders of the Ashton Grove congregation and well known throughout the community, was scheduled to lead the prayers of the people on the first Sunday of Advent. The Friday night before, his son Brett was involved in an accident that sent an elderly woman to the hospital in critical condition. Reid was called to the local police station at 2 a.m. to discover that his son had been driving while drunk, caused the accident, and would be held in custody to await a bail hearing Monday morning. The local paper carried the news in its Saturday edition. Reid and his wife, Julie, agonized over the entire incident. They felt embarrassed, ashamed, and angry at what their son had done and at the grief it created for the entire Davis family. At the same time, they felt deep concern for their son, his future, and the reaction of the community and the church family toward Brett—and indeed, the rest of the family. Reid and Julie hesitated to buy their groceries at the local store, wanting to avoid stares, whispers, and prying questions. Reid wondered if he should ask someone else to lead prayer at church the next day and even considered resigning from the eldership. How could he be a leader in good conscience while his son was facing criminal charges? Julie wept all of Saturday morning and wondered if she could even get through worship at Ashton Grove Church again. On Saturday afternoon, a knock at the door and the caring faces of friends from church led Reid and Julie to remember that their church was also family and was with them all through this crisis.

St. Paul's Church is worried and uneasy. Ever since the congregation replaced the ancient, beyond-repair organ with an electronic keyboard, Bert and Marjorie Sheffield have been absent from their usual places in the congregation of 28 members. Their absence was glaringly obvious. Marjorie had been the organist for 40 years before recently retiring. Everyone knew that the Sheffields were opposed to the purchase of the keyboard, but no one had anticipated that they might actually leave the church over it. Despite phone calls and a pastoral visit, Bert and Marjorie had not returned to worship; each Sunday produces another excuse for their absence. The anxiety level of this small church grows with every Sunday service and every weekday conversation among members.

Limited Vision

The efforts of those who participate in wilderness-survival programs pale in comparison to the determination of many a small congregation to survive the challenges it faces. A commitment to persevere can be a strength, but that same strength can become an obstacle when the wagons are tightly circled, allowing no change, no new leadership, and no variations to the established tradition. "Outside influence" can be seen as the enemy. Clergy in these settings may be merely tolerated, no matter how caring and perceptive they may be. "We've outlived all our previous ministers, and we'll outlive you too" is the grim code. On the other hand, "an 'old guard' that has controlled the church for years no longer has the energy or interest necessary for new programs, but is unwilling to turn the reins over to newer members. For pastors hoping to revitalize the congregations, the lay leaders' verbal assent yet practical resistance often breeds the tension that drives pastors out."[2]

> *Chuck and Sonya McGregor had been in ministry at Dundurn Church for just a year. Sonya had asked longtime member Regina White to sing a duet with her at the Christmas Eve service. During worship that evening, the "duet" became a "duel" as Regina did everything in her power to sing louder and hold notes a shade longer than Sonya. The veteran member was not going to be upstaged by the new upstart—even if Sonya was the minister's wife!*

Tradition easily becomes a powerful god in small congregations, a god whose demands are obeyed without question. With all its richness, tradition can also become a heavy burden to bear. Small churches may feel they must "carry on" with practices, groups, and committees to exhibit health, keep the legacy of their forbears alive, and perhaps even match the activities offered by larger congregations. The difficulty of viability in numbers is made more acute when practices and groups have outlived their original intention. Clergy and longtime church members alike often feel a profound sense of guilt when committees and organizations dwindle and eventually disband. Nostalgic and wistful references to "the good old days when . . ." may reflect deep discouragement. Members may struggle to find the motivation to strive for excellence and the willingness to accept the call to mission and ministry. Before this level of discouragement becomes systemic and overwhelms the church family, a realistic and welcoming adjustment to old ways can stem the tide.

> *Robertson Memorial Church was an impressive building that now housed 20 souls in the pews and a choir of four in Sunday worship. Each Sunday, the faithful four led the minister into worship down the center aisle as the faithful few sang the opening hymn. The choir's grumblings and discomfort with the procession were*

audible. "There are so few of us anymore, it just feels awkward to wander in with four voices weakly warbling a majestic piece of music like 'Crown Him with Many Crowns,'" complained one. "I think we just look plain silly—and I feel silly myself doing it!" said another. One morning, just before the minister led them in prayer, Larry Hamilton, the choirmaster, turned to Pastor Jennings and asked, "Do we have to process in? Couldn't we just go up the back stairs and straight into the choir loft?" The pastor saw no problem with that. There was an audible sigh of relief from the choir, and from that Sunday on, no choir entered in procession down the aisle at Robertson Memorial.

Limited Leadership

A deeply rooted tradition within the North American church is that worship is led by ordained clergy. Church members commonly believe this is the minister's job, a job for which he or she is paid by those same church members. Ministers have years of education that endow them with the title "worship expert." When lay leadership in worship is suggested, a common cry resounds: "But that's what we pay the minister to do!" Congregations that allow lay leaders to use their gifts, with an attitude that accepts and encourages this practice, must experience a cultural shift. Worship is reclaimed as the joyful calling of all God's people, who fully participate in every aspect of praise, prayer, and proclamation. For too long, worship has been seen as a "spectator sport," with "pew potatoes" watching the clergy "quarterback" the liturgy.

From the other side of the pulpit, the view is not much different. Clergy can feel strongly that worship leadership is their specialty. They may see lay leaders as intrusive, requiring more work in timely preparation, teaching, and rehearsal. Some clergy find it threatening to share leadership during worship. Other clergy may feel guilty, concerned that their congregations will see the presence of lay leaders in worship as the minister's strategy for doing less work.

Reg Thompson shook his head. The search committee was at it once again, interviewing a prospective new minister for Beech Trail Church. The candidate was strongly suggesting that she would want lay readers in worship. "Won't work," Reg said firmly. "Not that

I've got anything against people taking turns to read the Bible, but half the time you can't hear them when they stand up there. We'd have to put in a sound system, and I don't think we have the money to do that. You ministers are the ones trained to speak in public, not folks like us."

Pastor Marion Swift was delighted that the lay preacher in her two-point charge was delivering his first sermon. Randy had requested that he preach on a Sunday when Marion would be in worship. At the beginning of both services, Marion felt she had to explain: "I'm delighted that Randy Patterson is preaching his first sermon this morning. In case you are wondering, I didn't have a week off because Randy is preaching. He and I have worked closely together for several weeks preparing and honing his message."

Andrew Fredericks had been in the ministry for a while, but he had never gained a well-grounded sense of self-confidence. When his congregation at Marten Street Community Chapel invited a prominent lay preacher to lead services on Anniversary Sunday, Andrew felt uneasy. His discomfort increased when the service that day was dynamic, with a solid message from Scripture and powerful prayers. During the anniversary luncheon, one of Andrew's elders had approached him, indicating that she might like to get involved in leading worship. Over coffee with a colleague in ministry, Andrew confided to his friend, "I just don't like it. I went to seminary for years to become a minister. I'm trained for this. The pulpit is my turf. Besides, it'd be too much work teaching this lady how to do it. It's easier to do it myself, and then I know it's done right."

THE JOYS

One of the profound joys of the small church is the sense of home and belonging that holds its members deeply. Michael Lindvall, now pastor of the Brick Presbyterian Church in New York City, wrote a series of books during his time as a small-church pastor, telling the story of the Rev. David Battles and his ministry at Second Presbyterian Church in the fictional town of North Haven, Minnesota. After another day of pastoral visits and frustrations, David reflects on why he and his family remain at that small church:

> This is home because Minnie and a few hundred other people trust me to hold their hands should they die. It is home because Angus and Minnie dared to tell me the truth. It is home because old ladies reach out to touch our children as they pass by in church as if they were their own.[3]

Strength in Relationships

One of the obvious joys of being in a small church is that you are part of a family. Here people are known by name and know each other. Generations of families have deep roots and strong ties in some small congregations. In newer small churches, while the roots may not have had time to grow as deeply, the ties can be equally strong. Life stories are known, joys are celebrated, and sorrows are shared in intimate ways. Knowing and being known leads to strong relationships and deep bonds of caring, ultimately affecting every aspect of worship. Pastoral prayers include the specific concerns of family members. Awareness of needs and circumstances influence even the greetings before and after worship. The worship leader's familiarity with the context will color the time spent with the children, the illustrations and applications used in preaching, and even the celebration of the sacraments. Worship is not isolated from the rest of life, as relationships from church spill over into daily life events.

- A new widow attending church for the first time since her husband's funeral sheds tears during the final hymn. An aware and compassionate church family surrounds her with hugs and support following the benediction.
- A family whose fledgling store is destroyed in a town fire is lifted up in prayer during worship; family members find their burden eased as the church family finds tangible and practical ways to help and support them.

- Aware that a young boy's parents have just separated, the minister shows compassion, not surprise, when the boy shares that news as the children gather for their story time.

Worship in the small church is highly contextual and highly personal. David Ray, pastor of First Congregational Church in San Rafael, California, and author of a number of books on small-church ministry, offers a list of "Principles for Understanding Worship with Fewer Than One Hundred":

- Worship in smaller churches is a family reunion.
- Smaller-church worship is a time for social caring and building community.
- Worship in smaller churches is more emotional.[4]

Because interpersonal relationships matter in the small church, the style of worship is human and relationship driven. Worship is led in a manner more personal than professional. Small churches generally appreciate and accept sincere effort over perfection in performance. Worshipers in a small church seek to be personally engaged with, rather than entertained by, worship leaders. If "mistakes" occur during worship, if a note is missed or out of tune, if an item in the order of service is switched around, or an emerging situation necessitates an addition, small congregations are prepared to adapt. Because relationships matter more than performance, and because small congregations look for a "human connection" with their leaders, these "errors" can actually enhance family ties.

- The organist is ill on Sunday morning, and no other musician is able to fill in. The congregation proceeds to worship, reading the hymns in unison instead of singing them.
- During the celebration of the Lord's Supper, the last cup of grape juice is removed from the tray just before the last choir member is served. There is a brief pause in the service while an elder finds another tray and ensures that the choir member is able to participate fully in the sacrament.
- During the lighting of candles on the Advent wreath, a young child blows out the match with such vigor that the newly lit candle

is also extinguished. The congregation smiles and waits with loving patience as the candle is relit.

Strength in Tradition, Openness to Innovation

The small church is a multigenerational church. Whereas larger congregations offer a variety of worship experiences through Sunday mornings to meet different needs, the small church chooses another route. On first glance, it seems obvious that smaller numbers of people, resources, and timing in multi-point settings preclude different worship services. Yet another, even stronger truth motivates the small church: the members have no desire to "divide the family." It is more important that the family, regardless of age, live and worship together. Intergenerational learning happens naturally, as the older members teach by example how to hold the hymnbook and how to participate in communion, and the young offer energy and enthusiasm, and likely a new song or two.

Multigenerational worship leads small congregations to be adaptable in meeting family needs. For example, styles of music in worship have become battlegrounds in many places. Small churches can learn to sing both "Great Is Thy Faithfulness" and the latest contemporary praise song, and have done so with warmth and eagerness. It is apparent to us that change in many small churches is driven from two sides of the family: grandparents on the one hand and grandchildren on the other. Grandparents are not only willing but motivated to pursue changes and additions to worship that will keep their family of heritage and the family of faith together.

- After a youth-led service, an 83-year-old elder remarks to the minister, "Well, that wasn't my cup of tea this morning. But it doesn't have to be my cup of tea every Sunday. It was wonderful to see the young people in church."
- During a difficult time in her life, a 23-year-old woman discovers the hymn "What a Friend We Have in Jesus" and is eager to share this "new hymn" with friends.
- Three-year-old Matthew sits with his grandmother during communion. Surrounded by the faith family he knows and loves, he listens and watches and knows how to take part in sharing the bread and the cup.

In the world of music, every song has a melody. Once that melody is known, harmonies can be added to enrich the overall sound, from soaring sopranos to the rumbling of the bass line. In the small church, the melody of worship is known; there are established patterns and traditions of praise and prayer in the church family. This knowledge gives the opportunity for worshipers in small congregations, old and young, to add their harmonies—moments in worship that are creative and contextual. Once the melody is taught and understood, then improvisation emerges. It is the responsibility of leaders within the congregation to teach the truths of Christian worship and to establish theologically sound foundations for corporate worship. Then the harmonies and improvisations begin:

- A Lutheran congregation in the rural Midwest enjoys "bluegrass liturgy," with the familiar words of worship set to the indigenous music of the community.
- A Presbyterian church honors God as Creator each spring, in a service that blesses seed and soil, and offers prayers for the farm families within the church and in the area.
- An Anglican congregation in a small Ontario town does not have enough children for a formal Sunday school program. Instead, it offers a children's space in the sanctuary. During worship, children are free to engage in play or activities around a small table with chairs. Biblically based books, coloring materials, and safe, soft toys are readily available.

THE CHALLENGE AND JOY OF CHANGE

The addition of harmonies undoubtedly invites change. In the small-membership church, the ripples of change are profound. Since relationships are the bedrock of the family church, changes must be undertaken in a manner that respects this bond. Change that is well explained by trusted leaders has a greater chance of acceptance and success. As one of David Ray's 12 principles says, "It's folly they don't like, not change."[5]

In our experience, trusted leaders desiring to implement change as harmony to the melody are well advised to note that:

- The established melody (the worship history and traditions of the congregation) must be known and respected.

- Change should be motivated by a desire for the well-being of the family of faith.
- Change that is implemented on a trial basis gives everyone a fair chance to experience and evaluate.
- Changes must be explained clearly, with expectations outlined and avenues in place to express observations and impressions.
- Leaders need to allow for variations on their theme and to hear the improvisations and improvements other voices bring.

Leading change requires balancing commitment to the cherished traditions of a congregation *as it is* with commitment to the vision of what the congregation *could be* if the change were adopted. Leaders must recognize that the church does not belong to them and that it therefore should not be made in their image. It is not easy to walk this line, and leaders may lose their balance. The good news is that congregations can be remarkably forgiving of leaders who are prepared to admit missteps.

St. Anthony's Church had always left the task of ushering to a handful of men who served as elders and managers. In an effort to include the entire church, including women and children, in these responsibilities, the session decided to establish a rotation of families to greet worshipers at the church door on Sunday mornings. Unfortunately, this change was implemented before it was communicated to the congregation, resulting in hurt feelings and misunderstanding on the part of those who felt that their "job" had been "taken away" from them. It took some time and pastoral care to soothe the wounds. During this time, with careful communication from the session through the newsletter and from the pulpit, the reasons for the change were explained. Families do greet each week, and the move is now an established tradition—but it could have been better implemented.

In an effort to remove some of the distance between the preacher and the pews, Pastor Randy Grandis suggested moving the pulpit forward, so that it stood between the choir and the congregation. The leadership group, while in favor of the concept, was unable to visualize what such a change would look like, and so agreed to a trial period. The pulpit was moved, and it was announced that this change was being made on a four-week trial basis. Members with concerns or comments were asked to speak to an elder or the minister. In the end only two people expressed concerns, both indicating their support of the move but noting that they needed some time to get used to the change. After the trial period, it was agreed that the pulpit had found a new home.

SOMETHING TO GIVE

Small congregations are often seen as receivers rather than givers. They need help from larger churches, judicatories, and denominational officials. They require financial aid, need pastoral support during frequent periods between clergy, and seem to demand more energy from oversight groups than their size warrants. By focusing on the problems associated with small churches, lay leaders, clergy, and denominational officials undermine congregational self-esteem. Seeing themselves as a "problem" simply leads to more problems. A genuine appreciation for the strengths and joys of small churches leads to more possibilities. Keeping worship as the primary focus of small congregations in particular keeps such churches healthy and engaged in mission and ministry.

> *After participating in two gatherings to teach lay leaders in rural congregations how to prepare and lead worship, one man from a struggling church shared at the closing service: "I was discouraged and disheartened about my church, and was seriously considering leaving. These two events have given me hope that our church can live as we worship God."*

> *A small-town congregation, continually in a financial struggle, held many fund-raising events. One such event required the church to cancel its Sunday morning worship service to offer a brunch at the local arena. This pattern became an annual tradition. While this decision strengthened the congregation's bank account, it weakened the priority of worship for the church family. Worship appeared to*

be optional if more pressing concerns arose. Church attendance grew increasingly irregular, and a sense of discouragement invaded many. At another difficult point in their financial viability, the members wondered aloud about their future as a church.

In the same town, another congregation was discouraged and doubt-ful of its long-term future. Lay leaders and the minister looked at ways to renew worship; they implemented various changes that strengthened both faith and the sense of family. Worship atten-dance has grown several times over, and leaders continue to hold worship as a primary focus. The church looks to the future with hope.

A POSTLUDE

We believe that small churches have important gifts to *give* to the wider church. Chief among those gifts is their emphasis on and commitment to worship. Small churches do not offer a wide variety of programs, nor are they "hubs of activity" every night of the week. The main focus and purpose of the small church is to gather the family together for worship, Sunday by Sunday. It is worship that draws and keeps people. Worship is where voices lift in praise and prayer, and in conversation and concern with and for each other. This pattern, this focus, is one that needs to be reclaimed by the church of Jesus Christ.

The church exists to glorify God—a purpose that can be lost or muffled in a long list of programs, activities, and committee meetings. At a time when the need for congregational renewal is of paramount importance, and has spawned an array of literature, theories, programs, and conferences, churches would do well to recapture the essence of what the church is—a faith community that worships God. It is our convic-tion and experience that congregational renewal begins and lasts when it is rooted in worship. Worship is the foundation of small churches; wor-ship is something small churches can do well. Celebrating what small churches do well benefits everyone and glorifies God.

CHAPTER 3

TO GOD BE THE GLORY

Best Worship Practices in Small Congregations

As Tom Anderson slipped into the pew next to his aunt and uncle, he looked around the small sanctuary at Hawthorne Community Church and at the group that was gathering. He estimated that 15, maybe 18 souls were present for worship. He began to resign himself to the facts: this would not be a service anything like those at his own church. Tom's home church, New Hope Assembly, boasted three services on a Sunday morning, attracting a crowd of 500 at each worship experience. While one service catered to those with more traditional tastes, the first two gatherings featured the best and the latest in technology, music, and art. Tom preferred to go with his family and a few guys from work to the second service, where he was growing in his faith and found that his wife and children felt comfortable and connected.

But this morning, Tom was visiting his extended family, his Uncle Roger and Aunt Joyce Gilmour. They'd always been good to him, and he'd enjoyed staying at their farm as a child. So at least once a year, Tom came back to Hawthorne and to the Gilmour farm for a visit. Delighted that Tom had renewed his faith and was regularly going to church, Roger and Joyce were eager to have Tom attend church with them.

Hawthorne Community Church was a combination of three denominations, gathered together under one roof when it became clear that the tiny community could no longer support three churches. The amalgamation had gone quite well, as people were determined to make their "new" church a success. They shared a minister with the congregation in Lowden, a larger community about 20 miles west. The Rev. Amanda McClung enjoyed her min- istry with Hawthorne and Lowden and had passed the seven-year mark in her tenure.

As the congregation waited for Amanda's arrival, the organist played some familiar hymns, tunes Tom hadn't heard for years. "I Need Thee Every Hour" and "Blessed Assurance" provided a back- drop to the quiet conversation that surrounded Tom on every side.

"Why, Tom, it's great to see you in this neck of the woods again!" said Clayton McLeish, Tom's childhood Sunday school teacher.

"Joyce, you must be delighted that this handsome nephew of yours is in the Gilmour pew!" one of his aunt's friends exclaimed. Tom was warmly greeted; he appreciated the handshakes and smiles as people entered the sanctuary and found their places.

Tom glanced at the bulletin in his hands. The order of worship hadn't changed much it seemed. It was still neatly printed, indicat- ing what would happen when. No surprises here! The well-worn hymnals rested in their usual places in the pew racks, but were now sharing space with pew Bibles. Looking around, Tom was struck by the simplicity of the sanctuary, with no projection screens, no drum kit, no sound system, and no open platform. Instead, there was an oak pulpit, with matching oak hymn board, baptismal font, and communion table. "This will be a different worship experience," Tom mused.

The side door to the sanctuary opened, and in walked the Rev. Amanda McClung, still adjusting her robe after the car ride. With a smile she turned to the congregation, welcomed everyone, and led the group in a song of praise. The organist was joined by a guitar player, a young man who looked about 19, and the worship- ers lifted their voices in singing "Shout to the Lord." Tom smiled— it was a song they'd sung at his church last Sunday.

After worship, Tom joined in the coffee hour and conversation at the back of the sanctuary. It felt a little like coming home. That Tom was among the last to leave amused Roger and Joyce. On the way back to the farm, Roger began, "Folks were sure glad to see you, Tom." Joyce nodded in agreement. "And you know," Tom said with eagerness, "I was really glad to be there. It was a great service, Uncle Roger. Really great. The sermon was good, and Amanda was easy to listen to. I can see why you like her so much. It was good to sing some of the older hymns; the words have a lot of depth to them. I was surprised that you sang "Shout to the Lord"—we sing it at my church, too."

"Well, who'd have thought we'd be so contemporary!" Joyce said with a smile. "I don't know if it's so much about being contemporary as it is about worship. I just really felt like we worshiped God this morning. The prayers were really personal—I was really touched when Cameron McKay led in prayer. And the communion service was so intimate. I wondered if that's how the disciples felt in the upper room that night with Jesus." Tom's enthusiasm was growing. "Your church really knows how to worship!"

MAKING WORSHIP MEANINGFUL

In *Beyond the Ordinary: Ten Strengths of U.S. Congregations*, Cynthia Woolever and Deborah Bruce, of the U.S. Congregational Life Survey sponsored by the Lilly Endowment, the Louisville Institute, and the Pulpit & Pew Project, note that "Meaningful worship happens in congregations of all sizes. All congregations hold services where people feel joy and inspiration. These congregational strengths do not depend on size. But what predicts beyond-the-ordinary performance [in] meaningful worship? Two factors matter: congregations that have empowering leaders and worshipers who are growing spiritually."[1] Too often, the assumption prevails that small-membership congregations endure worship that is anything but uplifting and inspiring. How can enthusiastic, meaningful worship be generated among and led by such a small number of people? The answer to that question depends upon where one is looking. If our focus is on numbers of people, with "bigger" equaling "better," small churches lose out. But if our focus in worship is to glorify and honor God, then any and every size of church can worship well. Surely the focus of worship, as in all of life, is to "glorify God and enjoy Him forever" (Shorter Westminster Catechism, Q. 1).

The primary purpose of worship is to honor God, and to lift our praises and prayers to the Creator. Throughout any service, the prayers, hymns, proclamation of the Word, and celebration of the sacraments are means by which God's people glorify God. Contrary to the current social principle that "It's all about me," worship is "all about God." It is not about us. Therefore, the size, age, talent pool, church building, and technology available do not need to—and indeed, must not—define or motivate worship. As we stated in the postlude to chapter 1, we believe that as individuals, "we have no higher calling than to offer worship to God." It is in worship that human beings discover who they are created to be, and find purpose and hope in life.

These convictions are equally true for congregations, as their "highest calling," purpose, and hope are found in worship, in coming before God in praise and prayer. A congregation that loses sight of its primary purpose—worship—ceases to be a congregation and becomes some other social organization. Small congregations can and must focus on meaningful worship, as a matter not of survival but of faithfulness. Thankfully, meaningful worship is possible and is practiced in many small churches. These lofty ideals and theological foundations are expressed in worship that has a sense of purpose and direction. Just as a meeting flows better with a well-ordered agenda and an attentive chair, or a hockey team plays best with a skilled coach and a game plan all are committed to, so a worship service fulfills its purpose best when the congregation senses that the leaders are being led by the Holy Spirit and that they in turn lead the worshipers to glorify God.

Meaningful worship does not happen "by chance" but by the guidance of the Spirit of God through the Word of God. The Scriptures are a rich resource to guide worship. Within God's Word we find an order that enables God's people to fulfill their desire and duty to worship the Lord. For example, in the book of Isaiah, chapter 6, a profound moment of worship is described in connection with the prophet's call.

- Isaiah finds himself caught up in a vision, and beholds "the Lord sitting on a throne, high and lofty" (v. 1). A choir of seraphs sings praises: "Holy, holy, holy is the Lord of hosts; the whole earth is full of his glory" (v. 3).
- Isaiah is overcome by the holiness of the Lord, and by his own sinfulness: "Woe is me! I am lost" (v. 5).
- This confession of sin is followed by a reminder of God's grace and mercy, and a declaration of forgiveness: "[Y]our guilt has departed and your sin is blotted out" (v. 7).

- The Lord's voice is heard, issuing a challenge and a call to Isaiah. "Whom shall I send, and who will go for us?" (v. 8).
- Isaiah responds to the Lord's call, saying, "Here am I; send me!" (v. 8).
- Isaiah is told what the mission is, and he undertakes his prophetic ministry.

In this text, we see a pattern for worship that is faithful to Scripture and the leading of the Holy Spirit. This includes the "dance" or dialogue between God and humanity: God leads, we follow; God speaks, we respond. We have a sense of awe at who the Lord is; we have a sense of need as we recognize who we humans are in the presence of the holy Lord.

- When worshipers arrive in a sanctuary, they are in the presence of God. They are called to worship, and they respond with praise. These are the opening moments of worship: a call to worship, hymns and songs of praise, prayers of adoration or approach.
- Then, recognizing God's holiness and their own sinfulness, worshipers respond with a time of confession. The prayer of confession is an important recognition that we are in the presence of a Holy God.
- By God's grace, we are assured that our sins are forgiven. The assurance of forgiveness is a moment of grace and joy for God's people.
- The Lord speaks his Word to his people. In most churches, "The Word of the Lord" is read from Scripture, and then proclaimed via the sermon or message, drama, liturgical dance, and the children's time.
- The worshipers are called upon to respond with a faithful commitment to serve the Lord. In a service of worship, this commitment is expressed in our prayers, offerings, and hymns of personal and corporate commitment to discipleship.
- Our participation in the sacraments is a powerful response to God's actions, grace, and call. In some traditions, the Eucharist is seen as central to weekly worship; in others, the Lord's Supper is celebrated monthly or quarterly. In every tradition, and in every interpretation of the sacraments, they are intimate and compelling acts of worship.
- We leave the sanctuary to pursue and fulfill our calling as the people of God.

Unlike the Ten Commandments, this order of service is not carved in stone. Denominational and local tradition, the seasons of the church year, the specific theme of worship on any given Sunday, and the addition of other events in the service (e.g., welcoming new members, acknowledging special guests, celebrating the sacraments, or marking milestones in the lives of families or the congregation itself) may prompt a change in the order. This change need not be at the expense of honoring the movements and meaning of worship.

Moving from Plan to Praise

With many books, resources, conferences, and materials available to worship leaders, the importance of the small-church context must not be overlooked. "Small church worship is not large church worship scaled down."[2] While the principles of worship and the elements of worship are the same in large and small churches, how those elements are offered and led will differ between small and large congregations. As we have noted previously, the small church is marked by the bond of relationships and an atmosphere of intimacy. This is the place where "everybody knows your name and they are always glad you came." Sermons by a preacher perched in a pulpit high above the worshipers, a series of impersonal prayers, elaborate processionals and recessionals—these do not honor and respect the relationships and intimacy that are the hallmarks of the small church. Those entrusted with planning and leading worship in the small church must keep before them their context.

Worship planners must themselves be engaged as worshipers, not simply in packaging and delivering services. In planning, they must hear the voice of the Lord speak. The voice of the Lord must speak not only *through* the worship leaders but also *to* them. Leading worship is a demanding responsibility, not so much to achieve "a perfect performance," but to demonstrate, through an attitude of reverence and respect, that worship matters.

When speaking of "context" as an important factor in worship, we are not speaking simply of size. Context includes the history, culture, experience, and worldview of a particular group of people. In the Isaiah 6 text, for example, the passage begins with a very specific reference to the context. "In the year that King Uzziah died" (v. 1) is more than just a historical footnote; it is an indication of a time and place, a reminder of both the community's history and its present reality. Isaiah comes to this worship experience out of a particular context. So do those who worship in every church, large or small. It is critical that the context be reflected in both the planning and the leading of worship. Small-church worship leaders need to do as much exegesis of their context as of the Scriptures, and to be mindful of the life situations of those who will gather to worship God.

From a rural church conference in Australia, Christine recalls the following powerful story that was shared by a lay leader, Cathy. Cathy explained that the price of wool had plummeted by 50 percent in the early 1980s. The Australian government felt forced to make difficult decisions regarding wool production, a mainstay of the economy and a way of life for many. Farmers were offered subsidies based on the number of sheep culled from their vast flocks. It was a devastating time for farm families, as entire communities resigned themselves to reducing their livestock. Cathy related the events in her own family and farm community near Myrtleford, Victoria, in southeastern Australia. Her father and brothers conferred, and with a neighboring farmer decided to begin the slaughter. Bulldozers dug huge pits for mass graves, as sheep were shot and then buried. It was a sad, discouraging time for even the most hardened men and women.

The Sunday following the cull, Cathy, her family, and their neighbors gathered for worship at their small church. The texts for that Sunday included a reading from John 10, the famous words of Jesus Christ: "I am the Good Shepherd." In light of their own life experience, people wept as the text was read. But there was no mention in the service of the events from that community that week. No reference or acknowledgment was offered in the message, in the prayers, in any moment of the worship service. Cathy spoke of her grief and anger as she sat in church that day, a grief and anger not so much over what had happened through the week, but over what had *not* happened through the worship service.

Making Worship "Fit"

Worship is neither authentic nor meaningful if the realities of life, with its joys and sorrows, are absent. Worship leaders must not only be aware of the community around the congregation, but of the community that *is* the congregation. In a small congregation, it is not enough to know the individual life histories of the people who gather for praise and prayer. The culture of the small congregation requires that worship planners and leaders understand worshipers' personalities and preferences. Small congregations are not any more homogeneous than large ones, however, and not everyone will approach worship the same way. Corinne Ware, professor of ascetic theology at the Episcopal Seminary of the Southwest, builds on the work of the late church historian Urban T. Holmes, in describing four spiritual "types" of people, any and all of whom are likely present in congregations of 20, 200, or 2,000. Offered below is a summary of Ware's insights; readers are encouraged to read *Discover Your Spiritual Type* (Bethesda: Alban Institute, 1995) for a fuller discussion.[3] These insights are helpful to worship planners and leaders, not as categories or labels to isolate worshipers, but as ways to enrich and broaden the worship experience beyond the preferences of either the leader or the individual worshipers. Meaningful worship is not "comfortable" worship that "suits us," but worship that expands our knowledge of God, our faith and discipleship.

In the following diagram, we visualize the variety of "types" present in worship. The vertical axis represents a continuum of head/heart; the horizontal axis represents a continuum of "God is mystery/God is revealed." No one person is at an extreme end of either axis; rather, we are various shadings of any and or all of the quadrants. However, we do have a preferred type, a style or emphasis that we find most natural. Over time, people may shift among the quadrants, given life experience and growth in spiritual maturity.

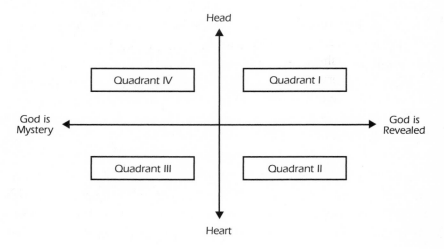

Quadrant 1 represents the way of the head. Individuals of this type prefer worship that feeds the mind and offers a hearty diet of intellectual nourishment for their faith. Sermons offer facts, history, and a call to a knowledgeable faith. Creedal statements, printed litanies, and hymns such as "A Mighty Fortress Is Our God," rich in content and historical imagery, are all appreciated.

Quadrant 2 represents the way of the heart. People of this spiritual type seek worship that touches their emotions, assuring them of God's love and compassion. Worship is enhanced by a sense of belonging to the family, the sharing of stories, and music and sermons that express and encourage feelings of joy, compassion, awe, and a personal friendship with God. A hymn such as "How Great Thou Art" addresses this spiritual preference.

Those who come to worship seeking silence, quiet music, periods of reflection, and well-known patterns in liturgy are represented in *quadrant 3*, the way of the mystic. Many worship services feel too wordy and noisy for these souls; they need time and inner peace to discern what the indwelling Spirit is doing. Prayers that allow silences, music that directs the worshiper to the God beyond our explanations, and a liturgy that uses an economy of language are the elements of their spiritual home. The music of the Taizé community gives this expression. Some prefer no musical background in times of quiet prayer or during communion.

Quadrant 4 gathers those who see worship as a way to active engagement in the name of the Lord. Sermons that summon worshipers to meet human need and to address political concerns, prayers that confront the struggle with principalities and powers, and music that stirs the faithful to devoted service or that proclaims the coming kingdom of God are desirable. Opportunities for hands-on involvement are crucial. Quadrant 4 worshipers delight in singing "The Summons" by John Bell as they walk to serve in the church's food bank. Even the physical posture of worshipers deserves consideration here. Kneeling during prayer or raising one's hands in praise can satisfy the desires of quadrant 4 people.

Worship planners in congregations of all sizes may find quadrants 1 and 2 the easiest and most natural places to begin—and often end— preparation. Their own worship experience and that of the congregation need not be confined to those types, however, and will, in fact, be deepened by the exploration and inclusion of both mysticism and activism. The small church has definite advantages in offering such opportunities to worshipers. Smaller numbers allow extra time to practice silence and to engage in reflection. Worship need not have a sense of "hurry," without choir anthems, soloists, and lengthy announcements to include in the service. It is simple to ask small numbers of people to move within elements of the service. For example, inviting children to gather for a story or asking others to receive the offering or to distribute communion can be carried out with little time or trouble. In small congregations, it may be easier and more natural to teach worshipers meaningful ways to experience the blessings of silence. In the small church, where worshipers have a strong sense of the congregation as a family, people are often open to experiencing silence if they understand that silence will benefit other members of "the household of faith." The small church can mobilize quickly, responding when particular needs or opportunities arise. Unable to engage in every cause, the small church is able to take ownership of one or two hands-on engagements in its community or the world. The entire community of faith will join the work of those activists within the congregation. Members will welcome and encourage information tables, hands-on activities, and invitations to participate directly in local school-lunch programs, to raise funds for development projects in agriculture and small business overseas, or to establish pastoral care teams. These focused concerns become part of the worship life of the congregation through specific and informed prayer and regular reports.

The quadrants can be helpful to worship planners and leaders. Understanding and being aware of the community that is the congregation strengthens leaders' efforts to provide God-centered, meaningful worship.

MEANINGFUL WORSHIP—STEP BY STEP

Worship leaders must remember their context, but they also need to provide content if worship is to glorify God and be meaningful. Whatever their type, worshipers desire services that have depth and purpose and that leave them with something to take home. Best worship practices include development of an overall theme, a "word from the Lord" that governs all the aspects and movements of worship. Worship planners need to spend time with the scriptures for this particular service of worship, and prayerfully discern "what the Spirit is saying to the church." We believe that worship leaders can serve best when a single theme is selected from the scripture texts selected for the day, either by the lectionary, the planning committee, or clergy. This theme is reflected in every aspect of worship, from the hymns to the prayers.

While small congregations have their particular styles, needs, and preferences, the best practices of worship planning and leadership transcend size. Worship is about God's glory and honor first and foremost. Whether 30 or 300 are in the sanctuary, common elements of worship practice should be present.

1. Scripture

As noted earlier, the scripture texts ideally discipline every aspect of the worship service. Thus, scripture must have a prominent place throughout. From the call to worship to the commissioning, we do well to draw on scripture. Calls to worship can be verses from texts that reflect the overall theme and that invite worshipers to consider the greatness and holiness of the Lord. Hymns can be based on scripture either directly, as in singing the Psalms, or in strong lyrics that quote or employ biblical images. Prayer language can be found in scripture. It is important that the assurance of forgiveness be from scripture, to emphasize the grace and mercy of God and not simply the worship leader's kindness. A children's time should involve stories from the Bible and not simply object lessons or entertaining talks. The sermon or homily is a proclamation of God's Word, not the word of the speaker. The offering can be introduced with scripture as a response to God's provision. Those who use a prayer book are immersed in the Word of God. As worshipers return to their daily lives, they may find both comfort and courage from God's Word, and in the phrase "Go in peace to love and serve the Lord" echoing in their ears, minds, and hearts.

Scripture is most often read by a solo voice, either clergy or trained lay reader. In addition to this tradition, scripture can also be read responsively by various combinations of individuals and groups. Thanks to modern technology, scripture may be projected on a screen, either in text alone or with images. Resources such as *The Gospel of John*, a film that remains faithful to the text but shows the story in a historically accurate, engaging way, can help worshipers receive God's Word with new understanding. Scripture can be acted out by members of the congregation, in either a "readers' theatre" or a short play. The stories and wisdom of the Bible can be told in song. Examples include the familiar "Turn! Turn! Turn!"[4] sung by the Byrds, or the music ministry of Michael Card, who has written songs based on much of the Bible, from Genesis to Revelation.

2. Sermons

Preachers, both ordained and lay, live between two worlds: the world of the congregation of which they are a part and the world in which scripture was written—scriptures that preachers are called to proclaim in this time and place. As John Stott, the noted Anglican theologian and preacher advises, preachers must walk the bridge between the context of the congregation to which they preach and the text of the Scripture that drives the entire worship service.[5] It is essential for the preacher to travel both ways on this bridge. The preacher goes as one commissioned by the congregation to travel from the congregation to the world of the text, there finding a word that speaks to the congregation. Thus the preacher crosses the bridge with all the struggles and concerns, all the hopes and joys of the congregation fully in view. As the research (exegesis) is done, and the text is struggled with, the preacher asks, "Where is there a word here for the people of this congregation? What word am I to speak into the midst of this group of people?" Having heard that word, a word that speaks first to the preacher, the preacher is able to return to the other side of the bridge, to the congregation, and there speak the word God has for this people in this place.

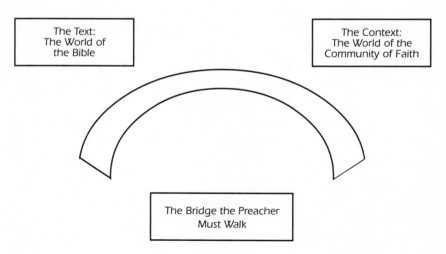

The Text:
The World of
the Bible

The Context:
The World of the
Community of Faith

The Bridge the Preacher
Must Walk

Two dangers confront the preacher who traverses this bridge. First, the preacher may never get all the way across the bridge, may not reach "the strange world of the Bible." The words spoken, no matter how eloquent, may remain but the musings of a gifted speaker, never taking on the power that comes from engaging the text of scripture. The second danger lies in the preacher's becoming so fascinated by learning about the text that the question "What does this say to my hearers?" is not sufficiently answered. The sermon in this case becomes a wonderful exploration of the text, an exploration that never speaks to the context in which the sermon is preached.

Walking the bridge, being faithful to the Bible and to their own context, is the task of preachers in all congregations. Sermons need to be true to the life of the congregation in which they are preached, using illustrations that engage the life experience of hearers, and making applications that fit the context of the congregation. Preachers must know their congregations sufficiently well to be able to answer with some accuracy such questions as: "How will Mrs. Smith, whose husband is in a nursing home, hear these words?" and "Will these words speak to Jeff Cleary, the lone 12th grader who comes to church faithfully with his parents each week?" The very fact that the preacher in the small church can imagine each of the regular hearers in such a way highlights the difference between preaching to 30 people and preaching to 300. This intimate connection between the preacher and the listeners gives the words of the preacher a powerful rootedness in the context. That power can also bring a limitation, however. Since the preacher can anticipate how Mrs. Smith and Jeff Cleary will respond to the sermon, he or she may be tempted not to speak the hard words heard on the other side of the bridge. The preacher may be afraid to speak with courage, "Thus saith the Lord." Just as the preacher in the small church must be aware of individual members of the congregation, so the preacher must be aware of the congregation as a whole. Those who hear the sermon are not just a collection of individuals; they are also a unique family unit, with a collective personality, experience, and tradition. Those who minister in multi-point settings can discern this truth quickly. Ross Stephens is pastor of Bridgeway Church, a small-town congregation, and Smither's Corners Church, a rural congregation. Ross prepares and preaches the same sermon in each place Sunday by Sunday, but he has learned that what the Bridgeway congregation laughs at, Smither's Corners will greet with

silence. It was only after his first year that Ross learned the reasons behind the differences: the Bridgeway congregation has remained stable
and strong over the years, and has opportunities for growth. Smither's
Corners, on the other hand, has a shrinking membership roll, and has
been asked by the diocese several times to consider amalgamation or
outright closure. Bridgeway looks at the present with joy and the future
with hope; Smither's Corners remains worried and tenuous over both
the present and the future. Worship simply has a different atmosphere in
each of the two churches. Questions the preacher must constantly have
in mind are "What is the word to this community of faith?" and "How
can I proclaim God's word in such a way that the worshipers can hear
what the Spirit is saying to their church at this time?"

If the preacher knows the congregation, the congregation knows the
preacher. In the small church, not only can the preacher not hide: often
there is nowhere to run. People know, or will find out, who you really
are. They will discern, or at least wonder about, their worship leader's
life, beliefs, opinions, likes, and dislikes. They will notice the way the
preacher relates to people, how much he or she cares about both individual members and the congregation as a whole. Small-town and rural
congregations will watch where their pastor shops, what social functions
and community events he or she attends; and they will talk among
themselves about how the preacher did at the funeral or at the community cemetery's Decoration Day service. Honesty, integrity, and genu-
ineness are key character traits for the preacher to develop and
demonstrate. In the small church, one's life often speaks more loudly
than one's words.

3. Prayers

"Prayer is the soul's sincere desire," says the hymn. Prayer must mark the
life of the church, large and small. In prayer, we remind ourselves that
life is not about us; rather it is about the God who lovingly called the
church into being, and who sustains the faithful in their mission to the
world. In prayer congregations demonstrate that they are a people who
"let go and let God."

Prayer is a way of communicating with an almighty and compassionate God. It is anchored in trust, in faith, and in hope. Prayer includes
both talking and listening. Corporate prayer goes beyond the individual

relationship with God. Prayer during congregational worship is at times spoken and audible prayer, but at other times it may be silent, as the community of faith listens together for the voice of the Lord and the leading of the Holy Spirit. Corporate prayer is not simply an individual offering personal prayers to God before an audience. Rather, in corporate prayer an individual is privileged to gather into words the life of the community within the sanctuary and beyond it, lifting those concerns, and thus those who pray, Godward. To lose this understanding of corporate prayer also loses the meaning and power of prayer in the congregation.

The pages of scripture provide a host of prayers offered by people in times of joy, gratitude, sadness, confusion, fear, anger, celebration, and concern. Meaningful worship includes all of these starting points of prayer. Worship leaders may find the tried-and-true acronym "ACTS" a helpful guide in preparing prayers for the gathered people of God:

A = approach and adoration
C = confession of sin
T = thanksgiving
S = supplication

A = Approach and Adoration. The prayer of approach and adoration begins worship. It reminds worshipers, as they come from the rough-and-tumble of their lives, to redirect those lives and thoughts toward God. This prayer is about God—God's grace, power, holiness, and presence. It is in this prayer that worshipers move from the rush to get to church on time and enter a sacred place and time: *"Be still, and know that I am God!"* (Ps. 46:10).

C = Confession of Sin. Coming before a holy God, we grow aware of our own unholiness, the sin that separates us from the Lord. That sin is both individual and communal, and needs to be confessed as such. In silence and spoken word, we come clean before the God who sees and knows us. The prayer of confession is more than a "laundry list" of misdeeds; it acknowledges our fundamental flaw: that as individuals, as communities, and as nations we prefer our way to God's way, our will to God's will.

Either in the body of the prayer or as a separate statement following it, worship leaders have the privilege of reminding the congregation that God is gracious and forgiving. This "assurance of forgiveness" is a crucial moment in worship, and reminds those gathered that *"If we say that we have no sin, we deceive ourselves, and the truth is not in us. If we confess our sins, he who is faithful and just will forgive us our sins and cleanse us from all unrighteousness"* (1 John 1:8-9).

T = Thanksgiving. Our response to God's presence and grace, the truth of God's Word and God's action in our world and call upon our lives, is gratitude. We offer thanksgiving during worship at various moments—in a particular prayer of thanksgiving, in the Eucharist, in the prayers of the people, and perhaps even as we begin and end the service. We thank God in prayer—for who God is, as well as for what God does. From creation to the cross and beyond, to our own time and place, we have received grace upon grace. In a society that demands rights and expects much, but offers little in the way of appreciation, the prayer of thanksgiving is a powerful reminder and statement that we depend upon God: *"O give thanks to the LORD, call on his name, make known his deeds among the peoples. Sing to him, sing praises to him; tell of all his wonderful works"* (Ps. 105:1–2).

S = Supplication. God's care and compassion are the foundation for this prayer, in which we bring the concerns of God's people to the throne of grace. In the same manner as the prayer of confession, the needs included in this prayer reflect both individual and corporate life.

The small church has a particular opportunity to gain a broader sense of itself in this prayer; the members become aware of and committed to the struggles and successes of the body of Christ and the world beyond the congregation's own boundaries. Realization of these connections makes the small church seem not so small, but part of the worldwide community of faith: *"First of all, then, I urge that supplications, prayers, intercessions, and thanksgivings should be made for everyone, for kings and all who are in high positions, so that we may lead a quiet and peaceable life in all godliness and dignity"* (1 Tim. 2:1, 2).

Preparing Prayers

Preparing prayers requires as much thought and care as preparing sermons. Worship leaders will benefit from exploration and use of the many resources available. The Bible itself is a rich source of prayers and prayer language, particularly the Psalms, the "prayer book" of the scriptures. While some denominations use prayer books as part of their tradition, all worship leaders would benefit from referring to and using this material themselves. This practice keeps prayers from becoming trite or repetitive, opening the leader to styles and subjects of prayer that take us beyond our personal limitations. Even extemporaneous prayer is enriched by careful thought prior to worship. We have found *The Worship Sourcebook*,[6] from the Calvin Institute of Christian Worship, to be particularly helpful in both prepared and extemporaneous prayer.

Prayers in a worship service may be expressed in various ways. They may be sung, spoken by a leader, read in unison, or said as a responsive litany. Times for silence and prayers directed by the "bidding" of the worship leader are meaningful.

Prayers must be rooted in the life experience of the community of faith, using the images and reflecting the joys and struggles that arise in any congregation. Prayer is more than listing all the community's challenges and celebrations, however, for in prayer the needs and hopes of God's people are brought to the God who hears and answers prayer. In prayer, especially prayer offered in times of great need, the church remembers again that life is not "all about us," nor is life under our control. The very act of prayer is a living lesson that life is about God, and is under God's guiding hand. While God is not "a tame lion"—to use C. S. Lewis's image of Aslan in *The Chronicles of Narnia*—God is good and compassionate and watches over all creation.

While not neglecting world concerns, the prayer of supplication in small-church worship is most authentic for worshipers when local needs are mentioned. They are, in fact, expected to be mentioned—if not by name, then most certainly in references to need. In the small church, a prayer request for "those in the hospital" will engender a particular name and face for the entire church family, even if that name is not mentioned. The danger of this kind of identification in prayer is that prayer requests may become an opportunity to collect material for the gossip mill, rather than to take those needs to the Lord, in whom any and every concern finds an answer. The goal of corporate prayer in the small church is not to let everyone know how Aunt Mildred is doing; the goal is to give Aunt Mildred into the hands of the good and loving God who knows far better than we do what Aunt Mildred truly needs.

Issues of confidentiality and community can easily collide in the prayer life of the small church. In large churches someone will know the person prayed for. In small churches most, if not all, will know the person prayed for. When members of the small church are in need, the community wants to know, and to know as many details as possible. If error or misinformation is passed on in prayer, a high percentage of the congregation may be affected, and the result may be to damage relationships among people who have frequent contact outside Sunday worship. Some wish to be prayed for by name in church; some may wish to be prayed for anonymously. Those leading in prayer at a communal service must answer the following questions:

- What does the individual or family want known publicly?
- What does the individual or family want made known by the worship leader during the service and during prayers?
- If the individual or family want information shared about the circumstance faced, what limits are to be observed and guarded?

How, then, can worship planners and leaders make wise choices about prayers at their church? We offer the following guidelines:

1. Every pastoral prayer (prayers of the people) should include an opportunity for people to name their concerns silently to God. They may be led to do so by the words of the worship leader: *"We pray for those who are sick and under a doctor's care." "We bring before you people who need your healing touch in their lives, physically, emotionally, and spiritually."* The period of silence following each request needs to be generous in length.

2. If a situation is truly common knowledge in the community, having been published in the local newspaper or widely discussed at the local coffee shop, it needs to be mentioned in the pastoral prayer. For example, a family's losing a home to fire, a death that shakes the community, a tragic accident, allegations of abuse at a local school—all these all need to be prayed for by a community of faith that is rooted in its neighborhood and community. Leaders must take care in these circumstances, as sometimes what "everyone knows" may not be that widely known after all.

3. If the pastor or lay visitor has visited the person or family, and has asked for and received permission to include the name in Sunday's prayer, then the person or family should be named in the prayer. The prayer will be further enriched if the pastor or lay

visitor has asked the family members what they would specifically appreciate the congregation's praying for on their behalf.

4. Prayer requests from family members or close friends passed on
to the one praying should be included in the prayer. There is no
need to go into great detail, or even for the one praying to know
much about the situation. Simple requests are appropriate, such
as *"We pray for Joan, that you would meet her need,"* or *"We lift up
Alec before you; please be close to him at this time."*

CHILDREN

Small churches often use their size and their lack of resources or facilities
to underestimate what they can offer children. We firmly believe that
small congregations can provide children with an excellent grounding in
the faith, a sense of belonging to God's people, and unique opportunities to participate in worship and worship leadership.

Children are worshipers, too—especially in the small church, with
its sense of being an extended family. Wise worship planners and leaders
will weave children into the preparation and experience of worship. The
presence and participation of children can be reflected in the design of
the service, with times for movement and change of pace; in the language used; and in the choice of music and worship materials. For example, music that includes a refrain or chorus is usually accessible for
children, even if the piece is unfamiliar. Children's concerns can be and
deserve to be included in prayer, with words that are profoundly simple.
The Worship Sourcebook provides prayers and litanies "especially mindful of children," such as this prayer used at Pentecost:

> God in heaven,
> You surprised and amazed Your disciples at Pentecost
> With the gift of the Holy Spirit.
> We praise You for the Spirit
> Who still fills our lives and hearts.
> Send Your mighty Spirit on us as we worship;
> Fill us with joy and excitement. Amen.[7]

Visual signs and symbols are effective with children. The colors of
the church year, the baptismal font or tank, the communion table,

the banners, and the stained-glass windows are all ways we proclaim the faith. There are probably symbols in every sanctuary that tell a truth: the carvings at the ends of pews may include a cross or a trinitarian symbol.

Children should be included in worship throughout, from the time of greeting to the final blessing. Children may serve in leadership roles as they are able—welcoming worshipers at the door, handing out worship materials, receiving the offering, lighting candles with their families, reading scripture, playing or singing music, and offering prayers. Children may participate in baptisms by carrying water, candles, and certificates. Older children may wish to help set the Lord's Table for communion, carrying the bread or offering a prayer. Some congregations that provide Sunday school during worship welcome the children back at the close of the service, allowing them to share what they have learned that day. These opportunities for children are best when an effort to rehearse, explain, and prepare them has been provided by worship leaders, Sunday school teachers, parents, or the pastor.

Many congregations continue to offer a "children's story" or "children's time" in worship. Contrary to the opinion of some, we believe that the practice of a children's time can be done well and can give children a definite sense of belonging to the family of faith. We hope the following points will help worship leaders craft children's times with integrity, respect, and depth.

- Keep the time short and focused. From five to seven minutes is ideal.
- This is not the "light entertainment" moment for the congregation. Treat the children with great respect. Laugh with them, not at them. Take their concerns and problems with the same seriousness that adult issues receive.
- Work with the children on their physical level—use a chair or stool, or sit on the floor with them.
- Know the names of the children; in a small church this is possible as well as important.
- Do not ask the children to do something you are not willing to do yourself. If you are not willing to wear a costume or touch something that might be "yucky," do not ask the children to do so.

- Be age-appropriate. In the small church a fairly wide age range of children may gather for this time. Children do not begin to think and make "abstract" connections until age 12. Stories and activities need to be concrete and experiential. Object lessons must be chosen with great care.
- Children's time is an opportunity to emphasize the truths of our faith: that God loves us as we are, and helps us grow to be all we can be. Stories and lessons must not assume negative, finger-pointing, or finger-wagging approaches. Positive and inspiring examples of faithfulness, kindness, love, and courage are welcomed.
- Do not be afraid simply to tell the stories of our faith. There are a host of children's Bibles and Bible stories available that will prove quite helpful. There are a variety of ways to tell the stories: puppets, skits, songs, modernized stories that present Bible principles. For example, the truth taught in the parable of the good Samaritan is to offer love and kindness to anyone, for we are all neighbors. Rather than explaining the original terms of "priest," "Levite," and "Samaritan," modern adaptations could be used—for example, "a minister," " a Sunday School teacher," and a woman from another country who wears different clothing and speaks with a different accent.
- Involve the children in the gathering, rather than making them passive observers. Even if one is reading a story, it is wise to stop frequently and ask simple questions (e.g., "What do you think will happen next?" or "Do you see the lake in the picture?") or to offer opportunities for children to express their ideas or feelings about what is happening in the story (e.g., "I wonder how Peter felt when he began to sink in the storm. How do you think he felt?") Beware of asking trite questions that are always answered "God" or "Jesus."
- Some seasons in the church year and scriptural themes lend themselves to a "connected series" of children's times. For example, Advent and Lent are wonderful occasions to build interest and excitement week by week, leading up to the events of Christmas and Easter. Try hanging an ornament related to the Christmas story on a Christmas tree each week, adding a star on Christmas Eve or Christmas Day. Use of the Jesse Tree, with its symbols of

Old Testament characters, is a marvelous way to connect the Old Testament with the story of Jesus. Simple skits can be used during a series on the Beatitudes or the Ten Commandments, reflecting God's character and actions toward us and suggesting how we might be encouraged to be formed by God's character in our own lives and relationships.

MUSIC

Few things engender more debate in worship than music. Few elements can set the tone or give expression to worship with the same power and depth as music. Our music and hymnody communicate more about our theology and understanding of faith than virtually anything else. This is an area to which worship planners and leaders will want to give due time and prayerful consideration.

In the small church, music plays no less a key role than it does in a congregation of any other size. The reality facing some small congregations is limited resources of both personnel and finances. However, quality and content need not suffer. Worship leaders need to know the resources available and to use them effectively. The use of computer-generated MIDI files and compact discs can provide accompaniment for hymn singing in worship. Middle judicatories can negotiate as a group and obtain copyright licenses that make music available at reasonable fees and avoid investing in expensive hymnals. Individual congregations benefit from copyright-license providers that offer fees based on worship attendance.

The content of hymns and songs must be congruent with the denomination's or congregation's theology, while the music must be accessible to the vocal range, abilities, and preferences of the worshipers. Some congregations appreciate classical music; others welcome "country" styles of songs and hymns. Some congregations can sing harmony; others require an easy-to-sing melody. Worship leaders can introduce something new or beyond the usual experience of the worshipers, but they must use the musical language of the community as the foundation.

- Music needs to fit the movement of worship. The opening of worship requires hymns and songs that lift the worshiper toward praise. Hymns such as "O Worship the King," "How Great Thou Art," and contemporary selections like "Shout to the Lord" or "Be unto Your Name" focus our attention upon God. The closing of worship invites God's people to service and mission; hymns such as "O Jesus, I Have Promised" and "Here I Am, Lord" fit the need, as do contemporary pieces like "Jesus, All for Jesus" or "The Servant Song."

- Music expresses prayer and reflection. "Make Me a Channel of Your Peace," "Be Thou My Vision," and "Open Our Eyes, Lord" are well suited to these times in a service of worship.

- Worship leaders must guard against using music that focuses excessively upon the "self" or that uses "I" language, as opposed to corporate language, such as "our" and "we." While there is place and time for individual reflection and commitment, congregational worship is primarily a time for the *community* of faith to honor God. In our highly individualized society, corporate worship and corporate expression are (and should be) countercultural.

- Most congregations, regardless of worship style, have a fairly restricted repertoire of music. New music gives fresh expression, challenges comfortable notions, and offers new insights into faith and discipleship. New music must be chosen wisely and introduced with confidence and care. Worship leaders and church musicians must prepare themselves well. Pieces new to the congregation can be brought in as a choir anthem or solo, can be played as an introit or offertory, or taught to the congregation by a song leader. It takes time for new pieces to be added to a congregation's "list"; new songs or hymns should be sung several weeks in a row perhaps, or sung regularly enough that they truly become known.

- Congregations may accept new pieces more readily if they are introduced at a particular season or occasion (Lent or a baptism or wedding), during the children's time, and if only one new selection is included in any one service. Some congregations include a "hymn of the month," chosen to fit the season or a series of sermons, that may be used in various ways or times in worship each Sunday in a given month.

- The family nature of the small church has its own internal guidelines for music. While a new contemporary chorus may not suit the senior elders, and a traditional hymn not be the preference of the teenager with an iPod and a laptop, both must be willing to include one another for the sake of the family of faith. Learning to appreciate a diversity of musical styles requires time, practice, and modeling by worship leaders. As with many other aspects of leadership, worship planners must both exhibit sensitivity to expressed concerns and show the courage to cast and implement a vision.

Sacraments

All of worship is about God's calling, God's doing, God's action, and God's presence. However, in some actions within corporate worship God is present and active in particular ways. These are "the sacraments." Whatever the traditions and theology of specific denominations, events in worship such as baptism and the Eucharist are crucial in the life and experience of the church family. Whereas much of this book has focused on what we as worship leaders and planners do, God is, in a unique way, the primary "doer" in the sacraments. Karla Wubbenhorst, faculty member at the Presbyterian College in Montreal, writes, "The reason that the sacraments are not just another act of the people's worship, and not primarily psychological in their effect, is because God uniquely says of them: '*I* am *acting* here.' . . . *God undertakes* these things."[8] In worship we respond to God through our hymns and offerings; we do these things for God's glory and praise. In the sacraments, we see God acting toward us out of grace and love, baptizing with the Holy Spirit through the sign of water, offering us the bread and the cup as signs of redemption and hope through Jesus Christ.

As instruments in the hands of a gracious God, worship planners and leaders have both the privilege and the responsibility to preside well. Sacramental ministry is undertaken with humility, thanksgiving, and a welcoming spirit. The use of appropriate gestures and warm eye contact with worshipers enriches baptism and the Lord's Supper. Familiarity with the words and actions is critical, so that constant reference to books and liturgies does not interrupt or impede the celebration. While celebrating the Eucharist with a thousand worshipers is powerful, it is profoundly intimate to celebrate the Lord's Supper with 20 you know by name and probably by need. While large congregations rejoice in the baptisms of tens of babies or believers, the small church rejoices in the baptism of Joseph and Clara's son, or the Hansens' granddaughter. An intimacy, a knowing and being known in the small church, gives the sacraments depth and warmth, and gives the worshipers a strong sense of belonging to God and to each other. The logistics of the sacraments in the small church need to be considered. These might include:

- At communion, the entire congregation can literally gather around the table or kneel at the altar rail together. There need not be a sense of hurry to receive the sacrament, as there is no long line waiting to be served, or great numbers of long pews around which to negotiate the movement of servers. At baptism, the family or believer can be physically as well as spiritually surrounded by the church family. Baptismal liturgies can be personalized with the names of the parents, sponsors, godparents, and the candidate to be baptized.
- Sanctuary space needs to be used well in sacramental worship and ministry. Even if worshipers are scattered at other times, worship leaders would do well to encourage a physical sense of connectedness and intimate space during the sacraments. The use of banners and the location of table, font, or baptistry can assist in creating the desired sense of community. Placing the furniture of worship closer together and surrounding that area with appropriate banners will give a sense of "enclosed space" in an otherwise cavernous sanctuary. Worshipers will be drawn to sit together or closer to the front when lighting and printed or projected resources invite them there.
- Since small-membership churches often have long periods of time between baptisms, it is important that the centrality of this sacrament not be lost by tucking the font away or using it for other purposes. Particularly in churches that practice infant baptism, the baptismal furniture can be hidden, and the sense of being a baptismal community can thus be forgotten. Every opportunity to preach about baptism and to renew baptismal vows is important.

WORSHIP IN OTHER SETTINGS

While the minister or worship leader may serve a congregation where 20 or 30 are gathered, opportunities for worship leadership arise where many more will be present. These include weddings, funerals, community services, Remembrance (Veterans) Day observances, and chapel services in hospitals and nursing homes. In all these settings, worship leaders may be tempted to speak in some generic form of spirituality rather than with a robust faith. While one need not be offensive or strident, worship ought to be led with conviction and integrity.

Weddings and Funerals

Weddings and funerals are not simply a duty to be performed. They are pastoral moments in the lives of families that are framed within a worship context. In small towns and rural settings they also become community events. Worship planners and leaders will serve well if they recognize these realities and preside with the awareness that people from non-churched backgrounds, skeptics, and the spiritually curious will be present. When the minister or worship leader is new, people will want to see and hear this person, assessing his or her personality and manner before, during, and after the service. Congregations also have something at stake here: they want to be proud of their minister, and they will look forward to a "good performance" at this public event. Sensitive and competent leadership is especially important in the case of funerals when the death has been particularly public or tragic. Such losses affect entire communities or neighborhoods in profound ways.

Prayers, hymns, scripture readings, and homilies need to be personal, yet they should also reach out to the community. In most small towns and rural areas, a "church culture" is still woven into the fabric of community life. People expect to hear such well-known scripture texts as Psalm 23, John 14:1-6, and 1 Corinthians 13. Those who gather for weddings and funerals also expect a personal flavor to the service—the bride and bridegroom need to be called by name by the minister, and addressed throughout in personal ways. At funerals, people want to hear stories about the deceased loved one. In both cases the worship leader will need careful preparation to be personal and yet not inappropriately familiar. Ministers do well to remember that the gathered congregation likely knows the couple, the deceased, and the family history much better than they do. Clergy need to balance the desire for "a personal touch" with the purpose of every service of worship, which is to glorify God. Weddings and funerals are public services of worship and must not be hijacked by personal preferences.

Worship in Secular Settings

Those who minister in small towns and rural areas have a particular opportunity to plan and lead services of worship in secular settings. With elements of faith still visible in these places, on such occasions as graduations, the opening of town and village councils, dedications of monuments, harvest celebrations, Remembrance or Veterans Day observances, and even community anniversaries such as "Founder's Day," people may still expect a prayer, a reading, and a short message from church leaders. While the prayer or message may only take a few minutes, time invested in preparing well for these events is well spent. One must be aware of the non-churched, skeptics, and spiritually curious who will be present, and of the expectations of the congregation if the worship leader is to fulfill this role with authenticity and awareness.

Hospitals and Retirement or Nursing Homes

Hospitals (especially chronic-care wards), retirement facilities, and nursing homes may also offer opportunities for services of worship. The sick, the active elderly, and frail seniors may highly value times for worship, and appreciate services that bring God's presence and blessing to them.

- Leading worship in these settings is a privilege and an honor, not a duty or a mere formality. In an increasingly secular society, public institutions need not offer religious services, but they often do so to serve their clients. Patients and residents who attend services do so out of faithful desire. These worshipers are at times of transition or crisis in their lives and in the lives of their families. Approaching such occasions with a sense of humility and respect will ensure integrity and provide a genuine opportunity to demonstrate care, compassion, and a sign of God's presence to people who may rarely enter a church for worship, or who are unable to participate in their own church.

- Planning these services requires time and careful thought. Research the context—who will be there? How long a time period is available? What resources are at hand—for example, music and printed materials such as hymnbooks or prayer books? Where will the service be held—in a multipurpose space, a dining room, or a chapel? Regardless of the location and the accessibility of songbooks, worshipers need to come to a gathering that honors God and invites their participation.

- The service should convey a message of encouragement and hope. Reminding people of God's faithfulness in the past and God's presence with us now and into the future is both appropriate and needed. Brief messages that contain a memorable story or illustration and leave listeners with something to think about are best.

POSTLUDE

Tom Anderson's comment that Hawthorne Community Church "really knows how to worship" is an attainable goal for any small-membership church. When worship is planned and led by those with an eye to "the Lord high and lifted up," the congregation is drawn to God and our ultimate purpose as human beings. As noted in the liner notes to Irish musician and worship leader Robin Mark's "Come Heal This Land" project:

> There is one thing we do on earth that we will continue to do in heaven. That is to praise and worship God. That is why we view life on earth, for those who love Jesus, as choir practice for heaven. . . . In light of that, there is no more important activity of the human heart than to praise and worship God. This is the reason we exist. This is our purpose.
>
> Michael Coleman, president, Integrity Incorporated

Whatever the context or occasion, worship is about God and God's glory. As God's people, we are richly blessed by God's patience, compassion, and justice. It is our high and holy privilege and calling to worship God and to lead others in that pursuit.

CHAPTER 4

RIDE ON, RIDE ON

Best Practices in the Multi-Point Charge

It's 8:30 on a crisp spring Sunday morning, and Dale Warren is on the road. Dale spends a lot of time on the road on Sundays, traveling to each church in her rural three-point charge. The first service is at Oak River, with a start time of nine; then Dale travels 20 kilometers, almost 13 miles, to Peters Corners for a 10:30 service; and she makes the final leg of her journey to Deerwood, 15 kilometers west, just over nine miles, for a service at noon. Dale has made this trek for six years, Sunday by Sunday. The pastoral charge has been together for 40 years, an arrangement born of economic necessity. The communities' population and financial decline led the three congregations to share a minister while keeping their own cherished buildings.

Oak River Church is the smallest of the congregations, averaging a dozen worshipers on any given Sunday. Church members are loyal and faithful, the descendents of Scottish and Irish settlers who arrived in the mid-1880s. The church stands on the corner of the McKibben farm. It is a modest wood-frame building erected in 1890, and would seat 75. Mechanization has reduced the number of farmers and hired hands needed in the area, a shift evident in the gathered worshipers at Oak River. Farming has changed dramatically over the years, with land holdings ever increasing in size. The congregation appreciates traditional worship and regular pastoral care.

The members are content with a quiet service of reflection and devotion and, while they mourn the absence of children in their midst, remain a tightly knit family.

Peters Corners is due north of Oak River, a small town boasting a population of 700. Dale lives here, in the manse next door to the church. Once a thriving community of several stores, four grain elevators, a school, and an arena for ice hockey, plus a Quonset building housing the local curling rink, Peters Corners has seen major changes in the last two decades. The school has been closed, with students now bused to Goodlands, a town of a thousand, 30 kilometers east (about 18 and a half miles). The grain elevators were dismantled in 1988. Only two stores remain on Peters Corners' main street, along with the post office, a gas station, the hockey arena, and the curling rink. Dale's congregation is located just off the main street, a brick building at the corner of Wilson Road and McMunn Avenue. St. Brendan's Roman Catholic parish, on the other side of town, is served by a priest who has six other parishes under his care. Peters Corners Community Church regularly attracts 35 worshipers each Sunday; it can have twice that number at Christmas and Easter. The congregation maintains a Sunday school of six and a Ladies Aid that claims a dozen members and offers several fund-raising suppers and teas throughout the year. This congregation carries the largest portion of the budget for the charge, and the members are aware of their responsibility for keeping things going.

Deerwood Church welcomes 20 worshipers through its doors each Sunday. Nestled in the hamlet of Deerwood, population 115, this congregation has weathered the cycles of drought in both farming and faith. Members are mostly retired farmers and their wives who have moved into town after passing the family farm on to their sons and daughters. The community has a tiny grocery store, a gas station, and an old school building that now serves as a place for community functions and a facility for a visiting health-unit nurse and a traveling library. The seniors in Deerwood have been actively lobbying for high-speed Internet access to reach their town. There is an energy in the congregation, evident in its weekly worship and fellowship potluck lunch. After three services and an early start to the day, Dale is grateful to share lunch with this congregation before heading home.

This year Dale has had the extra responsibility and joy of having a young theological student with her for a two-month immersion experience. Andrew Kim, a second-generation Korean Canadian who is passionate about his faith, is eager to engage in ministry, and seeks to broaden his understanding of the church in western Canada. Andrew's home congregation is Living Waters Church, a large downtown Korean congregation with two Sunday morning services—one bilingual, the other English only—to accommodate the 200 families affiliated with the congregation. While familiar with churches that have more than one service on a Sunday, and with services differing in content and congregation, Andrew is learning some of the unique opportunities and challenges of leading different services in different buildings and communities. As his experience draws to a close, Andrew is busy preparing a reflection paper for his professor of worship and liturgy at the seminary. On the drive back to Peters Corners, Dale invites Andrew to have a conversation about his paper.

"I'm dividing things into three major categories," Andrew begins, "the difference in congregational culture in each of the three churches, the struggles around time, and the disciplines of multi-point ministry for the worship leader."

"That sounds good, Andrew," Dale responds. "There are some unique challenges in this kind of ministry—challenges that I think you'd find in either a rural or city situation where one minister leads worship and preaches in two or more places." They continue driving and discussing, and soon are back in Peters Corners, and back to the realities of multi-point ministry.

Both Andrew and Dale have good insights into the nature of worship in small churches within multi-point or yoked arrangements. No two congregations are alike; time issues contribute pressures all their own, and worship leaders encounter particular struggles as they minister in this setting.

Robert L. Wilson, former director of the Ormond Center at Duke University Divinity School, notes that 50,000 Protestant churches in the

United States are part of a yoked (or multi-point) charge. These represent about one-sixth of total congregations. Yoked churches vary in size and location; some are small, rural congregations, while other yoked settings may include a large church sharing ministry expenses with a very small congregation.

VIVE LA DIFFERENCE!

Two or three congregations may share a minister, but that minister does not have cloned congregations. Each congregation has its own culture, heritage, community setting, traditions, expectations, experiences, and styles. All of these combine to form a particular group of worshipers, a situation requiring the worship planner and leader to make many choices about worship each week. "Do all the congregations receive identical services? Should I prepare services specifically designed for each place? What works here will not work there—how do I adapt?" Even the way the worshiping communities relate to the minister or worship leader will vary, a difference that unavoidably affects worship planning and leading. As Robert Wilson notes in his book *The Multi-Church Parish*:

> The local church is the institution in which the pastor has to work. Although a minister may have responsibility for several congregations, each is an entity. The temptation is for the pastor to perceive the parish as a unit when in reality it is two or more separate and distinct institutions. The person serving a multi-church parish is something like an expert checker player who plays several games at once. Such a player moves from one opponent to the next, making a move at each board. The games all have some things in common but each has its unique characteristics.[1]

Good worship planners and preachers do research and exegesis on biblical texts as they prepare services. Good worship planners and preachers will follow the same practice as they look at their congregations, and as they research and exegete—read out of—each place. They will ask themselves such questions as:

- What is the history of that congregation?
- What are the members' dreams and disappointments?

- What are their hidden values or core beliefs?
- What is the makeup of each congregation—age, gender, experience, and worship preferences?
- What is the "atmosphere" in each place—hopeful? Tentative? Discouraged? Joyful?
- Is the congregation in "survival," "maintenance," or "mission" mode?

As previously noted, worship is contextual. That context must be reflected in each worship service. "It is tempting to think that each congregation should hear the same sermon, to cut down on preparation . . . surely each situation is different and the needs of the people expected to be present not the same as elsewhere,"[2] writes David Cutts, a British Anglican priest. This is not to imply that a preacher conducts two or three totally different services, including two or three distinct sermons. While basic elements and themes are often the same in each service, differences will be evident in atmosphere, style, hymns, humor, and sermon illustrations. The physical surroundings and spiritual style make a difference. No two gatherings of 20 or 30 (or fewer) are alike. From one church to another, age ranges and gender proportions may differ. A story or a moment of humor may be added to or deleted from the sermon. One congregation may be open to prayers being sung; the others may find serenity in periods of silence. The way the children's story is presented may vary from one congregation to another. The wise worship leader will not necessarily prepare different services but will customize each worship experience to the context.

Just as no two congregations are alike, no two congregations face exactly the same issue in exactly the same way. Authentic worship will deal with the concerns particular to each congregation. The Rev. Esther Duncan was pastor of Cronin Memorial and St. Giles churches, a two-point rural charge. Cronin Memorial was grieving the loss of a patriarch, Ross Jamieson. His death had come as both a shock and a heavy burden to the congregation, as Ross was its wise council chairman and generous financial supporter; he knew everything there was to know about Cronin Memorial and the area. The Sunday after Ross's funeral, Esther preached a long-planned-for sermon on commitment to the people at St. Giles, but prepared a service and message of comfort, hope, and assurance for the Cronin Memorial church family.

Small congregations have some of the same issues and struggles as large ones, including times of conflict and the loss of church members. The size of the congregation will affect how these challenges are dealt with, however, if only because large churches simply have more "bodies" and resources than small congregations to cushion the blow. Any dissatisfaction, any loss of members brings pain, anger, and fear for the future that quickly moves through the congregation, affecting the entire body, not just the leaders or the small percentage of the congregation close to the problem.

A case in point: when three families left Taylor Junction Church because of conflict with the direction of ministry, a gaping hole was left in this small body of believers. The empty pews where those families once sat were sad reminders of recent events. The Rev. Bernie Norris had himself struggled with grief, anger, and discouragement over the conflict and the loss of these families. He felt fortunate to have St. John's as the second church in the charge. Things there were moving well. Bernie knew he had to speak to this crisis at Taylor Junction in some way, but he did not want to involve St. John's in a "family matter." An opportunity arose that afforded Bernie the time to write a message specifically for Taylor Junction, as the members of St. John's church were encouraged to attend an ecumenical celebration for the Week of Prayer for Christian Unity. Being relieved of responsibility for worship at St. John's that week gave Bernie the mental and emotional energy, as well as the time, to prepare a service that directly addressed the concerns of the other congregation. Bernie was able to participate in the ecumenical service, and then he proceeded as usual to Taylor Junction. He was able to lead a carefully prepared and sensitive service of worship, and then to speak about church conflict, taking his text from the Acts of the Apostles. People grew very quiet at Taylor Junction that morning. After the service, Bernie was warmly thanked by parishioners who commented that "this needed to be talked about," or said something like, "Thank you for speaking some wise words to us today."

Bernie avoided the temptation to "preach to the middle," to proclaim a message that would somehow suit everyone. The strategy of "preaching to the middle" avoids addressing a particular issue or concern that affects one congregation but not the others. This approach can result in blunting the edges of scripture texts and failing to be either genuinely prophetic or pastoral. Instead, on a week-by-week basis, the differences faced by each congregation can be respected in small but important ways in both liturgy and proclamation. This approach gives each congregation the opportunity to receive the encouragement and instruction needed for faithful living in its own context.

WHEN ONE SIZE DOESN'T FIT ALL

"Comparisons are odious." So said British playwright Christopher Marlowe (1564-1593). Leaders in multi-point ministry settings, take note! Congregations, leaders, and clergy must guard against comparisons, whether they lead to self-importance or self-deprecation, favoritism, or complaints. The larger or more financially affluent congregation in a yoked charge may develop a toxic pride as it carries greater responsibilities. The church family that sees itself as "smaller" or "weaker" can fall into another toxic trap, with the members seeing themselves as perpetually unable to measure up. The truth is that every faith community has areas of strength and areas where growth is needed. It is important that we follow God's call upon us, rather than seeking to be "better than," "different from," or "victims of" another congregation. Clergy must be particularly aware of any tendency toward favoring one congregation over another. Regardless of how one may try to disguise such attitudes, they will become obvious in the long run. "Rejoice with those who rejoice, weep with those who weep. Live in harmony with one another" (Rom. 12:15-16a).

In chapter 1, we told the story of John Elliott, minister at Hope Church and the congregation of Zion–Mount McConan. Hope Church was reluctant to use an overhead projector to provide the texts for congregational singing, while Zion–Mount McConan decided to proceed on a trial basis. Some conflict erupted at Hope Church over the issue, leaving John to face some difficulties. He is not alone; worship planners, leaders, and pastors will encounter such issues in any multi-point ministry. Multi-point ministry is akin to being the parent of two or more children. Wise parents do not favor one child over another; they would not deny offering Nathan hockey school because Clare didn't like hockey, or prohibit Clare from taking up the clarinet because Nathan showed no interest in music. The wise pastor or worship leader will respect the differences among the congregations without holding one church back from pursuing a particular worship style or experience. The key is in leading carefully and faithfully in each place. Here are helpful strategies for such leadership:

1. Communication between each congregation and its worship leaders must be clear, open, and respectful.

2. Leaders must carry out ministry in each context with enthusiasm and integrity, offering each congregation the sense that everyone is being treated equitably. This does not require that each church must be "equal" or the same, but that each church must sense that its worship leader or pastor is deeply concerned with its needs and committed to its well-being.

3. Congregations in general, and yoked congregations in particular, need to be aware of the intricate dance their minister or worship leader does with time management, overall workload, and professional skills. A new thrust in worship at one church will require extra time and effort (at least for a period of time) by ministry personnel. New initiatives need not take away from the other congregations—but can enrich those congregations' own lives, as their leaders are renewed and challenged and continue to grow, learn, and explore best practices in worship. Wise congregations, boards, and committees will respect the pastor's or worship leader's time and help him or her prioritize and use time wisely.

4. It may be both helpful and advisable to prepare separate bulletins or orders of service for each place, a practice not difficult in a computer age.

5. Pastors and lay leaders need to be reminded of the truths in 1 Corinthians 12:14-15, 27: "Indeed, the body does not consist of one member but of many. If the foot would say, 'Because I am not a hand, I do not belong to the body,' that would not make it any less a part of the body. . . . Now you are the body of Christ and individually members of it." Paul moves immediately from this discussion to speak of love: "Love is patient; love is kind; love is not envious or boastful or arrogant or rude. It does not insist on its own way; it is not irritable or resentful; it does not rejoice in wrongdoing, but rejoices in the truth" (I Cor. 13:4-6). Efforts toward unity in a multi-point pastoral charge are greatly aided by the practices of praying for each other, worshiping together,

avoiding "we/they" language, and sharing skills and gifts among the congregations. Worship leaders must act with courage and compassion, seeking primarily to be faithful to God's call and the leading of the Spirit rather than to make everyone happy.

6. Each congregation needs to designate people for the important roles of "communicator" and "go-between," which can be admirably served by well-informed lay leaders in each congregation. Worship committees will be stronger if they include members from all points within the charge. Worship bulletins or leaflets can include the concerns and activities of all the yoked congregations.

7. Pastors must guard against comparisons and complaints about any of the congregations entrusted to their care. Such comments will inevitably find their way back to the community and have a detrimental effect upon leadership and pastoral care. Even nursing these thoughts and attitudes will become evident in the pastor's practice of ministry. As Dietrich Bonhoeffer wrote in the classic *Life Together*:

A pastor should not complain about his congregation, certainly never to other people, but also not to God. A congregation has not been entrusted to him in order that he should become its accuser before God and men. When a person becomes alienated from a Christian community in which he has been placed and begins to raise complaints about it, he had better examine himself first to see whether the trouble is not due to his wish dream that should be shattered by God; and if this be the case, let him thank God for leading him into this predicament. But if not, let him nevertheless guard against ever becoming an accuser of the congregation before God. Let him rather accuse himself for his unbelief. Let him pray God for an understanding of his own failure and his particular sin, and pray that he may not wrong his brethren. Let him, in the consciousness of his own guilt, make intercession for his brethren. Let him do what he is committed to do, and thank God. . . . What may appear weak and trifling to us may be great and glorious to God.[3]

Bonhoeffer's words convict and challenge all who lead in ministry, and particularly those who lead in a multi-point setting, where the opportunity and temptation for comparison and complaint are particularly obvious.

While many multi-point ministries are located in small-town and rural areas, the practice of yoking congregations with one pastor is growing in urban centers. While physical distance may not be as great as in a prairie context, the distinctions among congregations, each located in different sections of the same city, may be just as evident. Father Rajeev Singh is priest at St. Thomas the Apostle Church in the east end of Newbury and serves the congregations of St. Anselm and of Our Lady of Mercy, also in Newbury. The churches are in very different quarters of this city of 250,000. St. Thomas is in a run-down section near the rail yard, St. Anselm is close to the community college campus on the west side, and Our Lady of Mercy is in the poverty-laden, downtown core. The congregations function differently and have different needs in worship and church life. "Father Raj" is well loved because he understands the differences, respects them, and serves his parish with compassion and commitment.

TIMING IS EVERYTHING—WELL, ALMOST

Anyone who has ever been involved with multi-point ministry is familiar with issues of time:

> "What time will our service be?"
> "We've always had the early service."
> "We prefer 10 a.m. and will lose members if we change."
> "I find it confusing to be switching times every few months!"

Those leading services have their own time issues—distance and driving conditions can exert additional pressures upon the preacher or worship team who must travel from place to place. If there is a baptism, communion, or a special event at one congregation, leaders must balance time constraints and the desire and responsibility to do things well, without cheating anyone or compromising on faithfulness and integrity. Time presents many challenges!

The issue of when worship begins in each congregation can be a source of conflict for everyone involved. There are no ideal solutions;

this is one area where the Christian community needs to learn and practice what it is to be Christian and in community. Each congregation needs to identify and clearly state its own requirements, but it must be just as concerned with the well-being of the other congregations in the parish. It may be best to have a minister or leader from another community moderate a meeting to discuss the concerns, to avoid any perception that the incumbent minister is swaying the decision or showing favoritism. Rotating service times, we believe, is fraught with difficulty. Particularly for newcomers or visitors to the community, service times and locations that keep changing present an unneeded obstacle to attendance and participation. Changing the service times may prove difficult for families in the church, as it constantly adjusts the "habit" of worship attendance.

An option to consider is training leaders for particular sections of worship. For example, Knox Church might begin worship at 9:30 a.m., St. Andrew's at 10:45, with a third point, Grace Chapel, worshiping at 11:45. It is impossible for one minister to be present to begin each service. Lay leaders can be taught to assume responsibility for the endings and beginnings of services, leaving the pastor time to slip away early and travel to the next point—while worship concludes at Knox and starts at St. Andrews, for example. This arrangement is not ideal, as it can break the flow of worship, and truncate any time to greet and talk with parishioners. But if time is a major irritant, everyone must make some compromises. In some settings this practice may need to be adopted only under particular circumstances, such as a service lengthened by a baptism or celebration of the Lord's Supper.

The challenges faced by the pastor or worship leader who does the traveling between services can be enormous. Not only does the pastor feel a burden to lead worship in a time-conscious manner; there are pressures related to the length of the service and the haste with which one must leave and travel. Pastors and lay leaders must address these stresses with understanding and compassion. At times the next church may have to exercise patience in waiting for the minister to arrive. Worship is important. It needs to be done well and it may, on occasion, require more time than the usual allotment. Clergy must exercise discretion and plan worship thoughtfully to avoid piling additional stress on themselves or on their parishioners. Worship need not be long to be faithful. Pastoral-care moments that might otherwise happen after worship must be dealt with respectfully and promptly. Solutions may include greeting people before the service, asking a trusted lay leader to record personal concerns, or offering times set aside to be present in that community during the week.

THINKING IT OVER

One of the major tasks of the pastor or lay minister in a multi-point setting is to gain familiarity with each place and to learn to distinguish the particular position the minister holds in a particular setting. Just as congregations vary in their worship practice, their perceptions concerning the role their minister plays may vary. In one congregation, the minister may be seen as "the sage on the stage"; in another, "the guide by the side." This perception influences how ministers practice all aspects of their calling, including worship planning and leadership.

Just as worship leaders exegete the biblical text, so must they "exegete" (read out of) each context and congregation. It is important to invest time and to listen carefully, reviewing the past and sensitively charting a course for the present and the future with a leadership style that fits well with each congregation. This task is daunting when a pastor is caring for one congregation or the other, let alone when also dealing with the interior shift that happens within minutes as the pastor travels from one place to the other on Sunday mornings. Leading worship is a holy calling, but also a heavy responsibility. Add to that task the transition that one needs to make between services, and the stress increases. Efforts to smooth that transition may include these:

1. Use well whatever time is available between services. Pay close attention to your own needs as you prepare for the next service. Debrief by reviewing the service in your mind or with a trusted traveling companion. This practice will assist the worship leader in learning from what has just happened, while necessarily leaving it behind to lead the next service freely. Pray for God's strength and guidance as you prepare to "do it all again." Eat or drink something to maintain energy levels, while avoiding caffeine or sugar-laden items. Listen to music as you drive to feel a sense of release, relaxation, inner peace, or renewed energy within. Keep focused on the purpose of worship: "to glorify God."

2. If something did not go well at the first service, assess what (if anything) might be done differently. You may wish to revise some wording, add or subtract an illustration, simplify a children's story, or shorten a hymn. This is not the time to rewrite an entire sermon, however. It is time to seek God's strength and help, and to trust that some part of worship—a hymn of praise or a prayer—may say more, and say it more eloquently, than any preacher could. Remember that worship is a whole, not just a sermon or a single piece of the liturgy.

3. If something has gone particularly badly and it can be left out the next time, do so. Consider it a learning experience, forgive yourself, and move on.

4. Traveling from place to place leaves open the potential to forget things—a children's story prop, sermon notes, an order of service, and so on. If possible, enlist the assistance of a trusted parishioner to help gather and pack all the necessary items during the closing hymn or while you are greeting worshipers. Preventing a crisis is better than re-inventing something in transit. It may even be wise to have an extra copy of the service, prayers, and sermon in the car. If something has been forgotten and cannot be delivered, the worship leader must adapt and do his or her best under the circumstances. The words "humility" and "humor" come from the same root, and both can be helpful attitudes under such circumstances. It may simply be best to admit your lapse in memory, laugh, and continue as best you can. Congregations often appreciate the humanity of their leader—and if they do not, this occasion provides a good opportunity for them to adopt this attitude. No doubt they can all recall having forgotten something, too!

A POSTLUDE

The call to "ride on" from congregation to congregation, Sunday by Sunday, is not a new one in the history of the Christian church. While the mode of transport has changed, the desire for people to worship God has not, even when those people are gathered in small places or in small numbers at significant distances from each other. Leaders of multi-point parishes can learn from the apostle Paul, an ardent traveler for mission and ministry. Paul taught the many congregations under his care to be concerned for each other. In his second letter to the church at Corinth, Paul wrote: "[Y]ou glorify God by your obedience to the confession of the gospel of Christ and by the generosity of your sharing with them and with all others, while they long for you and pray for you because of the surpassing grace of God that He has given you" (2 Cor. 9:13-14). Church leaders, pastors, and teachers in yoked congregations today would do well to follow Paul's example so that their congregations will, in turn, do likewise.

As Robert Wilson wisely observed:

> It is important to remember that the church has been called not to be successful in the development of its institutions but to be faithful in its witness and to minister in whatever situation it may find itself.... The multi-church parish is an institutional form requiring that each local congregation see itself not in isolation, but as part of the larger community of the people of God. . . . The multi-church parish requires close cooperation between the laity and clergy. This of course is necessary in any type of church, but it is particularly critical in congregations sharing a pastor. The lay members must assume more responsibility for the ministry of their church. The pastor must be willing to trust the laity to witness to their faith and enable them to carry forward the work of the church.... The small congregation that is part of a multi-church parish is going to be a prominent part of Protestantism for the indefinite future. They have been and will continue to be feasible organizations for carrying on the Christian witness and ministry.[4]

While Wilson's words are now over a decade old, they remain true not only for Protestants, but for the whole Christian Church.

CHAPTER 5

SAVIOR, LIKE A SHEPHERD LEAD US

Best Practices When There Is No Settled Minister

The Rev. James Matthews parked his blue Impala under a tower-ing maple tree on the north side of the yellow brick church. He was not the first to arrive that Sunday morning; two other vehicles in-dicated that the church was not empty. James grabbed his preach-ing gown and briefcase and headed for the oak doors of Edenbridge Presbyterian Church. A difficult task awaited him—to "preach the pulpit vacant" at this century-old church. James had never done this before; the Presbytery of Queen's Bush had appointed him as the interim moderator[1] for this congregation, yet another difficult task. His role would entail guiding the members at Edenbridge along the journey of self-examination as they grieved the loss of their much-loved pastor and looked ahead to their future ministry.

Today his ministry with them would begin, as the congrega-tion gathered to worship God and to hear the official presbytery decree read: that this church was now officially without a settled minister.

At the meeting held over lunch following worship, James met with the 21 men and women who remained despite farm chores waiting and spring planting calling. He began the meeting with prayer and then invited the congregation to tell him about the com-munity and church. The members knew that James was a city boy who'd been called to a town church 30 kilometers east (about 18 and a half miles) and so began with the basics of life in this farming district. Edenbridge had been settled by Scottish settlers in 1863. The land was good, and after the hard work of clearing the bush, farms sprang up and a community was born. Archie McKellar had donated three acres of land at the southwest corner of his farm for a school and a church. After a decade of work by Church of Scotland missionaries, construction began. The community took great pride in its achievements as pupils were educated and pews were full for Sunday services. Now the schoolhouse was long gone, but the church remained. The dedication of the founding families continued still, as familiar names were prevalent on the communion roll and the war memorial plaques on the church walls: McKellar, Walker, Cameron, and Sutherland. People with those surnames were present at the meeting with James and spoke with both pride and sorrow.

Robert Walker spoke first, standing to lean on his blackthorn walking stick: "Our church has a long tradition here. Stories abound about the old days when the precentor led the psalm singing, the minister preached for a good hour both Sunday morning and evening, and everyone learned the Shorter Catechism by heart." Murmurs of "aye" were audible, while heads nodded in agreement.

"But our community has changed so much!" said Margaret Cameron. "The farms are so much bigger, and while our own families have grown and gone, people from Belgium and Holland have bought up the land. They're mostly Catholics and have their own church in Dundee Valley. Now people are trying to make a living with tourist places, like the Sutherlands with their bed-and-breakfast and Willie Rutherford's rustic-furniture business. It is a pretty area, and people do drive through here on their way to the beaches on Georgian Bay. But it's all so different than it was, even when we were growing up."

Jean Walker spoke up: "Yes, and who comes to church now? The tourists don't, and with the community changing in size and who lives in the area, our congregation seems so small in a sanctuary that can seat 150!" Jean was known for her direct approach, and her statement reflected facts as well as perception. "So I suppose Presbytery's thinking about closing us down, are they?"

All eyes were upon James. He looked down at the floor, breathed a silent prayer for wisdom and began: "Well, there are some voices at Presbytery who feel that way. But not all. I'm still fairly new, and I want to learn from you and work with you as we look at the future for your church. I'm in no hurry, and I value your thoughts. What do you see for yourselves in the next, say, five years?"

There was a silence as the people took their turn at looking down at the floor.

Mary McCallum was first to speak. With a quavering voice, she lamented what seemed a bleak future: "There doesn't seem to be much hope for us. We had to work so hard to keep Reverend Galloway paid. The Women's Association is getting older and fewer, and I don't know how many beef suppers and bake sales we can keep on doing." Murray and Doris McKellar nodded in agreement; Doris wiped away a tear.

Robert struggled to his feet again. He thumped the blackthorn stick on the floor. "Now hold on! We can't just give up! We have a heritage here, a tradition to uphold! I for one am not letting Presbytery shut us down without a stiff fight! We've always had to work hard to keep going, both on our farms and with our faith. We've been through tough times over the years but kept going. We can't give up. What if your ancestors—or mine—had given up clearing the land? Digging the foundation for this very church? We'd be letting them down to give up now!"

Murray McKellar looked Robert in the eye. "I'm not one to give up," he said, "but you have to face facts. There's barely enough of us left to keep the building in good repair, let alone pay a minister's stipend. I love this place—it's in my blood. It was my great-great-grandfather gave the land. I want to keep the church here—but I just don't know how we can do it. I'd hate to see this building go to ruin; there's too much history here to let that happen!" Murray spoke with deep feeling, and there was a silence after his words.

"Well, what do you suggest we do?" Jean Walker looked to James.

James gulped. "Well, I'm not sure. I'm new at this. But I promise I will work hard to find some ideas for you to think about. Let's not assume that Presbytery is going to march in and close the doors. We can't be the only church facing this."

John McGregor had been silent up to this point. But now, he remembered something: "At my sister-in-law's church—she's out in Manitoba, you know—they were a lot like us. And they heard *about another small country church that was keeping on going but had ordinary people like us take turns at leading services and such. They couldn't afford a minister full time, you see, but didn't want to lose their church. So one or two figured out how to learn about preaching, and a few others took over the visiting."*

John's wife, Peggy, spoke up: "Yes, Ruth told me about it. And she said that they have a real minister come in a few times a year to do communion. She said the rest of the time, they have come to enjoy hearing their own people speak."

Jean Walker chimed in again: "Well, I'm not so sure I'd like to hear just folks like us, week after week."

Margaret Cameron responded quietly, "Well now, Jean, I think that there is something to think about here. Remember the two Sundays Reverend Galloway had laryngitis? Murray and Doris did a fine job, stepping in and taking over. It wasn't bad at all. We still had church!"

James spoke up: "Well, there are some ideas here already. I don't think we should turn off the lights and lock the doors yet by any means. Look, I've arranged for a variety of people to come on Sundays for the next two months. Some are retired ministers, and there are two lay preachers, one man and one woman, who will also take a turn each. In the meantime, why don't I do some investigating and report back to you in a month? How does that sound?"

With general agreement noted, James closed the meeting with prayer.

"Thanks for a good message today in church, Reverend Matthews," said Robert Walker, "and for being willing to stick up for us and help us." A smattering of applause followed the elderly man's heartfelt words, and a plastic container of sandwiches and a few cookies were tucked into James's hands as he made his way out to the car. "We don't want you to starve on the way home!" said Mary McCallum. "We need you to keep your strength up!"

Four Sundays later, James drove in to the Edenbridge Church parking area for an evening meeting. The tables in the small fellowship hall bore plates of cookies and pitchers of lemonade; the chairs around the tables were filled with the same 21 individuals who had attended the first meeting. After general chatter about fields, weather, and the progress of spring planting, James asked all to bow their heads for prayer.

It didn't take long after the "Amen" for all eyes to be fixed on James yet again.

James asked how things had been going. Nods and murmurs of approval greeted his inquiry. "We especially enjoyed that young girl—Sara Stephens—she had a good message and spoke loud enough for us all to hear," Murray McKellar said. James smiled to himself. The "young girl," Sara Stephens, was a 34-year-old teacher in his congregation—and a fine speaker, he'd discovered. Sara didn't hesitate when he asked if she'd travel out to Edenbridge. Then Robert Walker asked aloud the question that everyone was wondering about in silence: "So, young sir, what have you found out for us?"

"Well, Mr. Walker," James began, "I made a few phone calls, checked out some other small churches in a similar situation, and— as clergy are wont to do—I did some reading. And I do have some ideas to share. One of the best came from this book." James held up a glossy book titled Small Congregation, Big Potential: Ministry in the Small Membership Church.

Margaret Cameron eagerly leaned forward and exclaimed, "Why, I have the same book! I was talking with my nephew about our church, and he did some searching on the Internet. That was the same book he came up with—and he ordered one for his old aunt. It has some ideas I think might help us!"

James smiled at her enthusiasm. "It's a good book. Lyle Schaller is a church consultant in the States who's written many books. This is one of his newest. I've really enjoyed it, and wanted to read this part to you:

"During the past 50 years, American Protestants have accumulated a vast quantity of experience in (1) sending a part-time lay pastor in to serve a small church, (2) inviting a full-time minister to serve, and hopefully transform, a small congregation, (3) relying on seminary students to serve as the weekend pastor of one or more small churches, (4) asking a full-time minister to serve two or more churches, and (5) turning to semi-retired ministers to serve as part-time pastors in small congregations. The first four of these alternatives have produced a disproportionately large

number of short pastorates, dissolutions, mergers, disillusioned clergypersons and lay pastors, numerically shrinking congregations, adult children of members who continue to live in that community but have chosen a full-service church elsewhere for their family, and endless denominational financial subsidies, both direct and indirect."[2]

Margaret spoke first. "Does this mean what I think it means? That the old stand-by ways of maintaining small churches won't work anymore?"

James nodded in understanding. "Yes, Margaret, you've hit the nail right on the head." There was an audible sigh of discouragement around the table. Shoulders sagged and eyes looked down. Then Margaret spoke again. "So—that might also mean we're free to try something new?"

"Exactly!" James responded. "You folks have a long tradition of meeting challenges, standing together in tough times, and even adapting new things to suit your church. Now is another opportunity to follow in those footsteps. Schaller goes on to suggest that a team approach to ministry and leadership works best in small congregations facing transition. His thought is that a team of three to five leaders can minister most effectively in a small church like ours."

"But we can't afford one minister—how on earth will we afford more than one?" Jean Walker spoke her mind—a mind troubled by the thought of years more of fund raising and financial stress.

James shook his head. "Jean, I think I know where you're heading. I wouldn't even suggest that—but I would suggest that a few lay leaders and clergy guidance could give Edenbridge both a financial break and a way forward to the future. There are some gifted people right here—and I know Sara Stephens would be delighted to serve in some way."

"Well, that girl did give a good message," Murray McKellar said. Doris nodded vigorously in agreement. "I could listen to her again."

"Let's start thinking about how something like this might work," James suggested. "We don't have anything to lose by talking and thinking, do we?"

John McGregor agreed. "I think you're right, James. And if my sister-in-law's church could do it, I'm sure we can at least think about it."

The Edenbridge story is neither new nor unusual. Many small churches—rural, urban, inner city, and suburban—find themselves without a settled pastor and find their financial situation too tenuous to assure the stability needed to call a minister in the near—or sometimes distant—future. The obvious response is often closure—dissolving the congregation, scattering the flock to other churches (if they go anywhere at all), and selling the building to become an antique store or gift shop. While this may be the appropriate response at times, we contend that there are other avenues of hope to be explored. The mission and ministry of any congregation does not and should not depend upon clergy but upon the call and power of the Holy Spirit. Gifts and abilities are given to all God's people by the Spirit, including gifts and abilities in leading worship and proclaiming the Word of God. As Scripture teaches the church: "But you are a chosen race, *a royal priesthood*, a holy nation, God's own people, *in order that you may proclaim* the mighty acts of him who called you out of darkness into His marvelous light" (1 Pet. 2:9, emphasis added).

We have been privileged to learn from a variety of small congregations that lay-led worship and preaching can glorify God and nurture the community of faith. We offer the following model as a way to fulfill the call of God in small membership churches without clergy.

LAY WORSHIP TEAMS: A MODEL

Aware of a need and committed to the health of small congregations in general, and in our region in particular, we applied in 2000 to the Calvin Institute of Christian Worship, in Grand Rapids, Michigan, for a worship-renewal grant to train teams of three to five laypeople from eight congregations in southwestern Ontario. In April 2001, 10 teams gathered for a weekend training event. All but one of the teams came from congregations with fewer than 60 people in attendance on Sunday morning and with annual operating budgets of less than $50,000. Over half the teams were drawn from congregations that were without resident clergy.

Congregational leadership groups were asked to choose from three to five people in whom they recognized the gifts for worship planning and leading as well as spiritual maturity. In the selection process, leaders were invited to think of men and women of all ages and educational backgrounds. This approach resulted in the selection of team members

as young as 13 and as old as 75, bringing a rich variety of insights, experiences, and preferences. Teams were assigned a "coach" from outside
their congregation, whose task was to support, encourage, and guide the
lay teams in their preparation and planning of worship. The "coaches"
were to work with their assigned team for a year.

Over the course of the weekend, participants explored several aspects of worship:

- the theology of worship
- the order of worship: why we do what we do when we do it in
  worship
- outline of a planning process
- transitions in worship style
- children at worship

In addition, teams were given time to plan up to three worship services to be used in their home congregations within a six-month time
frame. Through the generosity of the grant, teams were provided with
the start of a worship resource library:

- a one-volume Bible commentary
- books of prayers
- a year's subscription to *Reformed Worship*
- resources on involving children in worship
- a large binder stocked with ideas and articles about worship and
  for use in worship

Through times of worship and fellowship, teams were able to build
community with one another and to build bridges to other congregational teams. Tired but energized teams returned home. When challenged
to tell one person in their congregation what the weekend had meant to
them within 24 hours of returning home, one participant said, "Did you
really think we *wouldn't* tell anyone about this?"

In September 2001 the teams gathered once more for a follow-up
weekend workshop. In sharing their experiences of planning and leading worship, participants commented on how much more meaningful
worship had been for them and how God had been present with them.
Presenters sought to address some of the concerns and questions raised:

- movement (psychological and physical) in worship, from praise to prayer, from adoration to confession, from pulpit to lectern, from message for children to message for adults
- writing prayers
- leadership flow from one team member to another
- use of music and introduction of new music
- discussion of contemporary worship

Teams were reenergized and refocused. A service of commissioning ended our time together, recognizing their gifts and calling to the ministry of leading worship. During this service, a man from a struggling small rural congregation without a pastor said, "When I came to the first weekend, I was prepared to give up on my church. These two weekends have given me the hope to keep on." His fellow team members shared this conviction and have since reported that the renewal of worship has been foundational to the renewal in the congregation.

Not only were the teams inspired; so were we. We were humbled that God would work through us, encouraging lay leaders to use their Spirit-given gifts. It is our experience that the gifts lay leaders have been given are remarkable. We were grateful that small congregations had a renewed sense of vision and life. Our conviction that worship is the heart of congregational life and the heart of congregational renewal was affirmed. And finally, it was evident that this is all about God and not about us.

TRAINING LAY PREACHERS: A MODEL

Participants challenged us to think about how we might teach them to preach. This request caused us to consider whether we should design a process for training lay preachers. In 2003, we again applied to the Calvin Institute of Christian Worship for a worship-renewal grant to train lay preachers from rural and small-town congregations in southwestern Ontario.

The content of the presentations included:

- the theology of preaching
- movement from biblical text to the "big idea" for the sermon
- movement from the "big idea" to sermon script

- the use of illustrations
- the preacher as person

In addition, participants were videotaped reading a scripture passage, and we reviewed the video with them. The lay preachers chose one of four proposed biblical texts and, with the study resources provided, spent time alone struggling with the text to develop a "big idea" for the sermon. The presenters were available during this time for questions and dialogue with participants. It was anticipated that the lay preachers would build on the work done during the weekend to write and preach a sermon within six months.

Once again the practice of assigning coaches was followed. Each lay preacher's assigned coach was available to help in the tasks of exegesis and sermon preparation. It has been and continues to be our experience that coaching plays a vital role in nurturing, refining, and encouraging the gifts of lay preachers. All God's people, ordained and lay, require accountability to remain true to scripture and the confessions of the faith.

Feedback from participants was again positive. They appreciated the resources received, which included a one-volume Bible commentary, a study Bible, a book of Bible maps and charts, a commentary on the Gospel of Luke (the gospel for the lectionary year), and a book on preaching. Many participants arrived at the event overwhelmed by the prospect of preaching. In written evaluations, participants noted that they had found through the weekend "that in fact we [learners] did have something to offer [could write and deliver a sermon]. It gave us confidence." Others noted the need to continue practicing their gift, to study the Bible and additional resources, and to be aware of the needs and experience of the congregation that would be hearing the sermon.

Approximately six months after the training weekend we gathered the lay preachers for a daylong refresher. We debriefed what preaching had been like for the participants, and then practiced the skills of exegesis, listening to the text and distilling a central theme upon which to build a sermon. Both presenters and participants found this refresher valuable.

These experiences have confirmed our conviction that the Holy Spirit gives to the individuals (lay and ordained) the gifts to lead worship and to proclaim God's word. We were grateful that participants indicated at every event that worship had become more meaningful to them (whether or not they were leading) and that they were more engaged listeners. Lay teams and preachers commented that all those who sit in the pew could benefit from being taught about the deep meaning and purpose of worship and the proclamation of God's word.

Return to Edenbridge

A choir of crickets surrounded James as he left Edenbridge Presbyterian Church after an evening meeting. James was doing a little singing of his own, for in his briefcase was the proposal for ministry put together by the congregation to be presented at next week's presbytery meeting. They'd worked hard, and James had enjoyed and learned much during the process. In a nutshell, Edenbridge Presbyterian Church was looking forward to the future with a ministry team of two lay preachers and a retired minister planning and conducting worship and a pastoral-care team of church members. Sara Stephens had agreed to preach one Sunday of the month. Murray McKellar agreed to attend a lay preacher's workshop and then preach one Sunday per month. Two Sundays a month would be led by the Rev. Owen Burch, a retired minister who lived in a small city 40 minutes south. Any fifth Sunday would be led by Margaret Cameron and the women's association. James would stay involved as the "coach," guiding the ministry team and meeting regularly with the lay preachers and pastoral-care teams. Much prayer, discussion, and investigation had gone into this ministry proposal. James was excited for this sincere band of the faithful, and hoped that his colleagues would be at least sympathetic to the plan.

James's trusty blue Impala found its way around the parking lot at First Presbyterian Church in downtown Ashton. Clutching his briefcase, James made his way into the large stone neo-Gothic church on the busy main street. There were no crickets that evening, just butterflies in James's stomach. At the call of the moderator, the meeting began at precisely 7 p.m. After worship and the usual preliminaries, it was down to business and soon up to James to present Edenbridge Church's proposal as part of the ministry committee report.

James began by describing the congregation, its history, demographics, and current health. He then passed out "The Edenbridge Plan for Ministry"—and asked if there were any questions. He didn't have to wait long. One by one the questions came, the concerns were stated, and objections were raised.

"I don't know about you, James, but I don't have the time to teach people how to do my job."

"More than that, I don't want to teach people how to do my job. I worked hard to get here—went to seminary for years, studied, took exams and wrote papers. It cost me a fortune, too, I might add. Why should these folks just waltz in now and take over?"

"I think this creates a new order of ministry. That breaks the rules of our denomination. Our presbytery can't just go off on its own and do this. And who are these people going to be accountable to, anyway?"

"I wonder if we're doing a disservice to these folks in the long run. Aren't we just creating a second-class congregation that will never have full-time professional clergy?"

The moderator stood up and called for order. He turned to James and said, "Do you want to take a moment to think through how you'll answer all these questions?"

James looked at his colleagues and said quietly and confidently, "No, sir. I'm ready now. We thought about these questions and concerns, and we have prepared some answers. I'd like to invite the representative elder from Edenbridge to join me—Mr. Robert Walker."

Blackthorn stick and all, Robert Walker approached the lectern. James made way, and Robert brought forth a carefully folded, neatly written piece of foolscap paper and began to speak.

"Edenbridge Church has been around for a long time—longer than you, and longer than even an old farmer like me. The church was a dream of the earliest settlers in our area; they longed for a place to worship their Lord. And despite many obstacles—and with a lot of plain hard work—that dream became a reality. Our church has a history of good times, and some lean years, too. But the longing to worship God has never changed. And isn't changing now. I know some of you think it'd be easier if we just gave up. You wonder why we want to keep going in our little church. I don't know how else to say it other than it's in our bones to worship and to be a church family. We've faced change, we've faced difficult times before this—and through our determination and God's faithfulness,

*we've carried on. This time is no different. Just our plan for minis-
try looks different. We believe in God and in ourselves—that we
can continue to worship at Edenbridge; the word of God can still be
preached and his praises sung. And that's what matters most. I'm
asking you—we're asking you—not to deny us the opportunity to
pursue the same dream our great-great-grandparents had: to worship God in the community where we live, with the folks we know
and care about."*

Robert looked up at the presbytery, and with a thump of his
blackthorn walking stick said, "I hope you've heard me." Then, carefully folding his paper and returning it to his inside suit-jacket
pocket, he moved aside and motioned for James to return to the
lectern. The moderator thanked Mr. Walker and then invited James
to continue.

"I think Mr. Walker has stated well the feelings and determination of the congregation, which are behind this proposal. Ultimately, we have a congregation that simply wants to continue to
worship God and be a church family—and are willing to give of
themselves to make that happen. I have heard the concerns of my
colleagues—and while I understand them, I find myself disagree-
ing with them. It is my understanding and conviction that we ministers of Word and Sacraments are also called to be teaching elders
—'to equip the saints for the work of ministry,' as Ephesians says. I
also believe that the Holy Spirit gives people, ordained and lay, the
gifts to plan and lead worship and to proclaim God's Word. I'm not
convinced that laypeople are taking 'jobs' from ordained clergy—
they are following God's call for them and for the encouragement
of God's people."

The presbytery clerk spoke up. "But what about this concern
regarding a new order of ministry? Some of my colleagues in other
denominations are wrestling with the polity required for new categories of ministry."

"Well, I think we need to look around at what other denominations are doing." James replied. "And yes, the Anglicans and the
Roman Catholics are using lay leaders in a highly sacramental
tradition—lay leaders who lead worship and preach. But we don't
have to look outside our own tradition. I'm no church historian,
but the earliest Presbyterian clergy had large circuits that took them

sometimes months to travel around. The laypeople continued to gather weekly to worship, sing praises, and listen to God's word read and expounded. For example, on Prince Edward Island, Presbyterian clergy were able to visit Presbyterian congregations only in the summertime because of the challenges of travel. The clergy baptized the babies born in the previous year and celebrated the Lord's Supper and then returned home, leaving lay leaders to preach and lead worship. These lay leaders and congregations understood that they were accountable to the presbytery. The proposal from Edenbridge is consistent with our history and past practice.

"As to whether this model does a disservice to small congregations, it seems to me that it would be a greater disservice to close down a church where people gather to worship God, listen to the Word proclaimed, and engage in mission in their community and beyond. Maybe we need to listen to what the Spirit is saying to the church today: a 'real church' is not defined by having a full-time minister but by how the people of God worship God, witness to their faith and work with each other."

When James had finished speaking, there was a pause. And then John Smith, the representative elder from Killarney, another small farming community, stuck up his hand. When recognized by the moderator, he stood to his feet, and said, "My question is for Mr. Walker. I know that I would be very uncomfortable preaching in my church; the people know me too well. They know about my family, my farm, everything—they will think I am saying that I am better than they are if I were to preach."

Robert Walker responded, "I wondered the same thing when the Reverend Matthews and our church started talking about some of us doing the preaching. But we're there to listen to God's Word, aren't we, and not just the words of any person, ordained or not. Besides, even some of the best ministers I've known had their faults—and I still heard God's message. All of us are sinners, aren't we? If I remember my Bible, I think Paul talked about being 'the chief of sinners'—and he sure preached. Used his life and his sin as an example of how great God's grace is. There was another hometown preacher that people questioned at first because they knew him and his parents—Jesus of Nazareth. I think it is a daunting responsibility to preach—but I believe God can and does use ordinary folks to get his message across."

The room fell silent as Robert Walker's words made people think and consider again what was before them. The moderator thanked both Robert Walker and James Matthews and asked the presbyters if they had any further questions or comments. Finding none, he proceeded to ask for the vote on the ministry plan for Edenbridge Church. Although not unanimous, the motion passed. James smiled and Robert shook his hand, and they returned to their seats. James sighed and breathed a short, silent prayer of thanks—and hope that now this would all work for the Lord's glory and the good of the folks at Edenbridge. A new dream was becoming a reality.

WHAT WE'VE LEARNED ALONG THE WAY

The Edenbridge story is fictional, but based on facts. Along the ways of our own ministry experiences and the worship workshops, we have encountered congregations and individuals who find themselves in this very situation. The practice of lay-prepared and lay-led worship has enriched these churches and enabled them to continue in faithful worship and witness. Among the things we have learned are:

1. We have been enriched, too, in working with and encouraging gifted laypeople who have a deep hunger for meaningful worship and a deep love for their small congregation. The Holy Spirit's gifts of proclamation and prayer are in no way limited to the ordained, but are powerfully present in and through the whole people of God. To repress those gifts is to deny the providence of the Spirit.

2. After every workshop, in every place, we are humbled and thankful that people continue to tell us that they have become better worshipers themselves by learning about worship preparation and leadership. Those who have been taught about preaching tell us that they read the Bible in a fresh, new way, and have gained skills in listening to and thinking about the sermons they hear.

3. It has been exciting to see laypeople gripped by the biblical texts, as they explore and experience what "the Spirit is saying to the

churches." Their hunger for solid biblical understanding and their recognition that worship is rooted and grounded in scripture form not only their church life but also their personal lives as disciples of Jesus Christ. They learn to look at and listen to life and the events around them with the eyes of faith and to adopt values and actions that reflect their love for God and God's Word.

4. In follow-up workshops, we have noticed a growth in skill and confidence in worship teams and lay preachers. Practice and experience are great teachers, and with a coach alongside, the truths of scripture, theology, and worship are kept in view. Lay preachers grow in confidence as they exegete biblical texts; lay worship leaders mature in preparing prayers, reading scripture, addressing children, and understanding the theme and flow of a service. This experience benefits the lay leaders and the preachers themselves, but it also benefits congregations. As people experience the deep meaning and purpose of worship, they are confirmed in faith and encouraged with hope. The size and situation of the congregation need not define or discourage them; instead, they can be set free to worship and engage in ministry.

While our ministry experience has been in small-church settings, it is our conviction that churches of every size would benefit from teaching, and using the gifts of, laypeople. If we are truly "the body of Christ," then as Paul taught the Christian Church in Rome, "[A]s in one body we have many members, and not all the members have the same function, so we, who are many, are one body in Christ, and individually we are members one of another. We have gifts that differ according to the grace given to us" (Rom. 12:4-6a). The story of Edenbridge, and the many Edenbridge-like congregations in North America, is not a new one, nor one that will not be experienced by others in the future. The future for small congregations and their ministry of worship can be rich and life-giving as they glorify God.

A POSTLUDE

Having read the Edenbridge story, you may have recognized yourself and your congregation. If so, please use the following as starting points for your own story of transformation.

1. Are key congregational leaders aware that the present ministry model is not sustainable? It is essential that members of the congregation sense that change is necessary.

2. Ministers or judicatory leaders can encourage lay-led worship by including lay leaders in worship: reading scripture, offering prayers, and leading the children's time. Preachers can plant seeds by their choice of illustrations and by affirming the role of laypeople in all aspects of church life.

3. Worship workshops can take on a variety of formats, from a weekend conference-style event to a series of evening or Saturday gatherings. These events can be offered in a single congregation or multi-point charge, or within a wider grouping of congregations (such as a presbytery, synod, or diocese).

4. Potential workshop leaders are present within easy reach of most congregations. Those planning such events need to ask:

   - "Who are good preachers—ones who can teach others to preach?"
   - "Who leads in prayer with passion and might share that gift with lay leaders?"
   - "Who relates well to children in worship and might provide guidance to beginners?"
   - "What printed or recorded resources or training events are available from our own denomination, from religious publishers, or organizations like the Alban Institute?"
   - "What resources might be gleaned from the Internet?" (*Caution:* Careful discernment required!)

5. Leadership in the form of mentoring and coaching plays an important role in the renewal of congregations. Faithful listening, empowering, guiding, providing resources, sharing the workload with the leaders already present, speaking out, and providing others with the opportunity to speak are critical tasks God's Spirit can use in the work of transformation.

CHAPTER 6

O BREATH OF LIFE, COME SWEEPING THROUGH US

A Model for Tomorrow's Small Congregations

The coffee and cookies served by the Sandy Fork Church Ladies Aid were a welcome break in the midst of the Rocky Lake Presbytery meeting. Over in one corner of the church basement, Charlie Osborne, Carol Hansen, and Judy Dixon were deep in conversation. All three were ministers, and all were increasingly concerned about their extra responsibilities caring for congregations without clergy.

"Well, the next item on the agenda is one I've been dreading." Carol sighed. "With Jack Collins resigning from the Little Doe River Church, one of us will be asked to assume pastoral care and leadership responsibilities there. I wonder who it will be?"

Charlie shrugged his shoulders. "I've already got more than I can handle with my own two churches, plus Marble Trail and Whitesburg. It had better not be me!"

Judy's "Don't look at me!" retort turned the attention of the group back to Carol.

Carol asked the question they were all thinking: "What on earth are we going to do with these small rural churches? Clergy don't stay long, the congregations tell us they're struggling financially, and all of us have more than enough to do with our own churches, without having two more. I don't blame Jack for moving on, but it sure makes it harder for the remnant left behind!"

As Charlie, Carol, and Judy emptied their coffee cups, the voice of the moderator, Dan Engle, rose above the gathering: "On behalf of Rocky Lake Presbytery, I'd like to thank the ladies for the coffee and cookies. Homemade, I might add. It was great. Thanks so much." Applause was offered by the small crowd, followed by audible groans when Dan cheerfully continued: "And now, brothers and sisters, let's get back upstairs and back to our meeting."

Rocky Lake Presbytery and ministers like Charlie, Carol, and Judy are not an isolated example of the challenges facing small congregations and the clergy who serve them.

FACING THE CHALLENGE, FORMING THE FUTURE

All churches must look to the future, to discern God's call and to shape their witness and worship accordingly. Small churches too must look to their future, and take hold of the challenges, opportunities, and tasks that await. In this closing chapter, we do not presume to offer the final word on all small-church ministry but instead to offer some foundations, some challenges, and some dreams about the future of worship in the small church. Despite a world that grows increasingly infatuated with and gauges success by large numbers, there is a particular place for small-membership churches. Carl Dudley of Hartford Theological Seminary notes in *Making the Small Church Effective:*

> In a big world, the small church has remained intimate.
> In a fast world, the small church has been steady.
> In an expensive world, the small church has remained plain.
> In a complex world, the small church has remained simple.
> In a rational world, the small church has kept feelings.
> In a mobile world, the small church has been an anchor.
> In an anonymous world, the small church calls us by name.[1]

In cities and rural communities, small churches can thrive. These congregations offer something that larger churches cannot: a "culture-contrasting" community of faith that will draw some people. As David Ray, a pastor who has served small churches, notes, "We've [small churches have] often tried to be what we are not and forgotten to be what we are."[2]

Small congregations remind us of what matters most in this life and the next: worship and faithful relationships. Healthy small congregations remind us of what is truly enough in a consumerist society always seeking more. Loren Mead of the Alban Institute reminds us that while the small church

> is *not* always beautiful, it is enough. Small is enough. It is enough for keeping on. It is enough for faithfulness. It only takes two or three, Jesus said. Most small churches have at least a dozen or two. Small is enough for holding lives and families together and making a contribution to a community. It is enough for breaking bread and sharing wine, for wrestling with the scriptures, for calling one another to new life. It is enough for praying, for following Jesus. What else do we need?[3]

Small congregations remind all Christians to rejoice in God, who provides the "enough" necessary for the community of faith to worship and witness.

Small churches exist in many contexts: inner city, suburbia, small town, and rural settings. While we have particular experience with rural congregations, we believe that all small churches can and should look beyond their membership rolls, church walls, and community contexts as they worship and serve God. Small congregations are not private clubs but part of the worldwide Christian church. They are called to be aware of and involved in the broader concerns and challenges facing the church of Jesus Christ. Addressing these issues influences how we worship and how we respond to God's call heard in worship. In their book *Rural Ministry: The Shape of the Renewal to Come,* the authors, members of the Rural Church Network of the United States of America and Canada, offer the following challenge:

> We believe that God is calling rural churches to a new vision, a transformation of character that is evangelistic, missional, and deeply satisfying. Rural ministry confronts the central challenges of our era: the changing world economic order, the globalization and questionable sustainability of the world's food supply, the environmental crisis and controversies, racism and migration, equitable access to social and public services, and—most centrally—the question of how we can live together as a community.

These are not simply social questions, they are questions addressed to the churches of Jesus Christ. They are congregational and theological questions. In short, the challenges of our time are deeply spiritual and will involve religious answers. God is calling rural parishes to be witnesses to the resurrection, to promote reconciliation between enemies, to care for the life of the world, and the salvation of our own souls and those of all others.[4]

While this challenge is addressed to the rural church, clearly all churches are called to witness to the resurrection, to promote reconciliation, to care for the life of the world, and to seek the salvation of all. These central purposes of the church begin in worship, are sustained by worship, and find their culmination in worship.

A TENTATIVE MAP OF THE SMALL CHURCH

It is dangerous to say anything about the future shape of congregations, for God has a plan and a design for the church, and God also has a tendency to surprise us. With humility, therefore, we offer a sketch of what small churches may look like in the future.

- Small churches will arise and be sustained in diverse locations. Geography, ethnic demographics, and sociology all play a part in the composition and style of any church; the small church is no exception.
- Small congregations will continue to be a reality in rural North America, some sharing clergy and other staff in yoked or cooperating relationships, others without settled ministers.
- Small congregations will arise in inner-city contexts, as various linguistic groups seek to provide worship in their own language.
- Some midsized congregations will find themselves becoming smaller, as the effects of a post-Christian culture erode church attendance.
- Churches will find niche markets—for example, some offering traditional worship, while others may provide worship in a country-western style.

- Still others will grow up around very focused ministry opportunities, such as working with people with intellectual or physical disabilities.
- Small congregations will have wide-ranging leadership models.
- Traditional multi-point or yoked congregations may share clergy.
- Individual congregations may be served by part-time ordained ministers.
- Congregations without ordained clergy may be led by a single trained lay leader.
- Congregations without clergy may be led by a team of lay leaders.
- Leadership may be shared by all within the congregation.
- Small congregations that cannot sustain weekly worship, yet retain historical significance (if only in their own community), may be under the overall care of another parish, and gather for worship at particular times or for an annual "homecoming" service.

With this variety of locations and models of ministry, a tenacity of spirit, and a commitment to the community of faith, the small church is here to stay.

While the context and shape of the small church may change, the reality is that the small church is not going away. Since the small church is here to stay, it is incumbent upon church leaders at the congregational, middle judiciary, and national levels to move from simply reacting to the challenges facing small-membership congregations. It is important that these leaders take the initiative to support small congregations in their worship and witness. In *Transforming Congregations for the Future*, Loren Mead prescribes nine congregational needs.[5] While Mead directs these toward middle judicatories, we believe that they apply to every level of leadership. A summary of his observations follows:

1. Congregations need help when they get into trouble. The church family needs help to see clearly the root of the trouble and a strategy to deal with it.
2. Congregations need to be left alone. Small churches need to feel that they are trusted to carry on their ministry and that they are not the subject of continual microscopic examination.
3. Congregations need to be held accountable when they are off base.

4. Congregations need pastoral care in times of loss, moments of celebration, and the marking of milestones.
5. Congregations need pastoral care for their pastors, to encourage clergy who may feel isolated or "unsuccessful," and to provide help in times of heavy stress.
6. Congregations need help with leadership development. This help is particularly crucial for small-membership churches, and it requires delivery in ways that meet the needs of small congregations.
7. Congregations need technical assistance such as how to plan, how institutions work, and how to discern the times in which we live.
8. Congregations need a sense of their place in a larger mission. Small churches need to be encouraged to widen their horizons as they ask, "Who is our neighbor?"
9. Congregations need someone who listens and listens and listens. Small congregations need someone outside who listens and pays attention enough to understand them.

While Mead looks at these issues from an administrative standpoint, we contend that each of the statements above can apply equally to worship life, for churches in general and for small churches in particular. For example, small congregations benefit from being held accountable to denominational doctrine and best practices in worship. Such accountability strengthens congregational identity and helps in the effort to feel "connected" to a larger community of faith (statement 3). Small churches doing ministry and mission with predominantly lay leaders would profit from focusing on Mead's sixth and seventh points. This style of ministry seems to be a viable way forward for small-membership churches, which need effective leadership, but which also grow best when worship is led well. Skilled worship leaders are developed and educated and have access to well-written resources. Mead notes the need for churches to gain a sense of their place in "the big picture" of world Christianity (statement 8). In worship, through the choice of hymns and the content of prayers and sermons, small churches can gain a vision of their place and part in God's plan for the church and the world.

Both judicatories and congregations must be forward thinking, not reactive, about the small churches in their midst. Leaders must help congregations seize with vigor the opportunities provided for worship and witness, rather than "trying anything and everything" when congregational health is rapidly declining and death is imminent.

"SEE, I AM DOING A NEW THING"

Throughout the history of the church, technological advances have helped shape congregational life, including corporate worship. In the past the introduction of electric lighting and the widespread use of the automobile altered congregational worship. More recently, audiovisual equipment and computers are changing the way worship happens. Technological developments have the potential to modify the ways small congregations worship. A wide range of innovation is taking place in some contexts. Of course, not every practice is suitable for every congregation.

1. Small-membership churches often have difficulty finding people with the requisite musical skills. The CD player offers an alternative to the church organist or praise team. Some hymnbook publishers have produced CDs of accompaniments that can be played to support congregational singing. In other congregations, the gathered community sings along with one of the many available praise-and-worship CDs. Since with CDs it is possible to jump from one track to another rather than having to fast-forward and reverse a cassette tape, the worship planner can use music that fits the service theme with ease.

2. Upon returning from worship conferences, many leaders of small churches wonder how they will ever be able to develop drama teams to enrich worship in their own congregations. The willingness of various professional drama teams not only to publish scripts but also to produce video versions of the sketches allows congregations without drama teams to bring the power of drama into their worship life.

3. Multimedia presentations no longer require the local congregation to have a technologically capable member willing to spend hours preparing a four-minute piece. Through resources available for download from the Internet, small congregations have access to the same high-quality productions that much larger congregations make use of.

4. Sermon time is a challenge for many small-membership churches, a challenge that some are addressing through the use of technology. Videotaped sermons are readily available and can be used in worship. With the advent of Internet streaming, congregations with high-speed capability can have a sermon preached live in their midst, even though the preacher is many miles away.

We are aware of the risks that technology poses to the small-membership church. If it becomes dependent on the resources developed with large congregations in mind, the distinct strengths and challenges of the small congregation are lost. Sermons especially must be rooted in the reality of a particular congregation in a particular place. Worship planners and leaders must exercise discernment when choosing among the resources technology brings so easily to hand. The first question to ask is not the technical one: "Can we make this work?" Rather the question should be: "Does this fit who we are and the worship and witness to which we have been called?"

An important way to encourage and support small-membership congregations is to hold up alternative ways of "doing church." We dream of the day when the members of a congregation will say, "We want to be a church that has a vital mission and ministry, and we, the laypeople, will lead that mission, starting with worship." To do that, those who take the initiative will look around the congregation and find in their midst a retired schoolteacher, a small-business person, a stay-at-home parent, and the mechanic from the town garage—people who share a love for the Bible and a gift for speaking the Spirit's word to the church. Supported by the congregation and with the blessing of the middle judicatory, including the incumbent minister (if any), these individuals will be among those called to preach, developing a rotation that fits the rhythms of their lives. Since worship is more than preaching, and also includes prayer and praise, the congregation will identify people who are gifted worship leaders and others who are inspired to pray aloud on behalf of the congregation. These people will be called out to form teams of worship planners and leaders. They will not simply read a scripture passage or read a prayer someone has handed them. These lay worship leaders will plan and prepare worship services, including prayers and sermons. The congregation whose worship is so led will consider itself blessed to have such gifted and committed worship planners and leaders in its midst.

Such a vision challenges the prevailing models of church experience, calling for a more collegial understanding of ministry in which lay and ordained work together, celebrating the gifts of each. In this model, harmonious working relationships between clergy and laity are built not on separate spheres of responsibility but on a shared commitment to worship and witness, tasks to which both clergy and laypeople are called.

If lay leadership is to succeed in small-membership congregations, clergy will play an important role. Clergy adept at small-church ministry will be those skilled at mentoring, coaching, drawing out, and equipping men, women, and youth to recognize and use their God-given gifts in worship leadership. The ministry of those ordained to Word and Sacrament is not threatened by lay ministers. Lay leaders can free clergy to attend to aspects of ministry often neglected amid the myriad of demands placed upon pastors.

This partnership in ministry will have a far-reaching impact upon how clergy themselves understand their calling and are educated to exercise it. While clergy use much of their time preparing worship and writing sermons, the calling goes beyond these tasks. Central to this conviction are the words of Ephesians 4: "The gifts he gave were that some would be apostles, some prophets, some evangelists, some pastors and teachers, to equip the saints for the work of ministry, for building up the body of Christ" (vv. 11-12). Pastors have the task of "equipping the saints for the work of ministry"; preparing and educating lay leaders is a crucial part of the minister's call and responsibility. Attending to that responsibility will assist clergy in worship planning, sermon preparation, and teaching as more lay leaders respond to God's call for *their* work of ministry.

If clergy are to be effective in equipping the saints, changes in their theological education are needed. Traditionally, pastors have been taught the art and science of worship preparation and leadership as a "solo" activity and as their domain of expertise. This style of training for ministry tends to result in clergy with a "lone ranger" understanding and practice of ministry—qualities that do not serve well those congregations where 20 or 30 gather. As these congregations are here to stay, the wise seminary faculty will look to the needs of congregations and reformulate the methods and concepts of theological education to prepare men and women to serve those needs. Teaching about worship will be infused with an atmosphere of partnership, and the notion of mentoring and coaching gifted lay leaders will be seen as normative, not exceptional.

From their discernment of the call to ministry to the completion of their studies, clergy need mentors. Mentoring is often "caught" rather than "taught," best learned by experience rather than by textbook. Seminary studies could advance the concept of collegiality and mentoring by classroom and fieldwork experiences that are relationally based, not simply didactically focused.

Glen Sawchuk was both excited and apprehensive about his call to River Rapids Church. The small congregation was located in a beautiful community of a thousand people, surrounded by forests, lakes, and mines, more than 700 kilometers (434 miles) north of the Canada/United States border. The nearest church or community was 150 kilometers, or 93 miles, west. Glen was delighted with the warmth and commitment of the congregation. However, he soon realized that ministry was not something he could effectively do alone. The times when Glen was away—on a much-needed vacation, taking study leave, or attending meetings in the south—left the congregation without worship leadership and with no pastoral caregiver for times of crisis. Glen saw the needs, as did the congregation. Glen also noticed that some in the church family were particularly gifted in praying, in studying the Bible, and in caring for others in difficult times.

With "equip the saints" ringing in his mind and heart, Glen set about what would become a hallmark of his ministry in River Rapids. Calling together a few people, Glen began teaching them about the meaning and purpose of worship and the basics of preparing prayers and constructing sermons from studied biblical texts. After meeting with the group for a few weeks, Glen invited these people to lead the worship service in a month's time, when he would be attending diocesan meetings in a neighboring province. In the weeks preceding the lay-led service, Glen reserved time to meet with Joanne, who would be preparing and preaching her first sermon, and with Ray, who would give the children's message. He also spent time with Oliver, who was leading the prayers for worship. In those meetings, Glen took on the role of a mentor or coach—encourag-

ing, guiding, listening, and at times offering thoughtful challenges when "teaching moments" arose.

Joanne struggled with the scripture she'd chosen to focus on— a favorite story from her childhood, Matthew 19:16-30. Jesus's encounter with the wealthy young man seeking eternal life had had a deep impact upon her faith. In her draft sermon, the issue of giving money and possessions away figured strongly. Concerned that the message might be too narrowly focused, Glen asked pointed questions of Joanne and the text: "I like what you have to say about material possessions, but do you think this story is only about money? What do you want your hearers to take away with them, or be motivated to do after worship? Withdraw their savings? Or look at the depth of their commitment to being Christ's disciples? Or something else?"

Ray needed help in making the children's story more suitable for the young children. "The kids love you, Ray, and they'll be eager to be there with you. Just remember that they're all pretty young and need something really concrete to focus on. Is there a way that they could help you tell the story?"

Oliver had developed good themes in the prayers. Glen told him so and then commented, "When I lead in prayer, I try to remember two things. I need to pray the prayers, not read them. Second, I need to make sure that there is enough time for people to bring their thanksgivings and requests, their hopes and fears into the prayer. That means praying slowly and offering times of silence that they can fill." Glen felt confident that the worship service would go well as he left River Rapids to attend the meetings. He also knew that one of the first things he would need to do when he returned home would be to get together with the three to talk about how the service had gone.

What Glen (and we) discovered is that mentoring is more art than science, more about walking alongside people than standing in front of them, dictating every move. The image of the coach is an appropriate one. In the world of sport, the coach does not play the game. The coach helps the players develop a love for the game and excellence in playing it. In the world of lay leadership in worship, the role of the pastor is like that of the coach: encouraging people to develop a love for God, excellence in leading worship, and the gift of inviting others to worship God. The recovery of the pastor's role as "spiritual director" gives us hope for a renewal of the role of "equipper" or "teacher" for clergy today.

PRACTICAL CONSIDERATIONS OF LAY LEADERSHIP

As we have spoken about this vision of lay worship leadership, the comment is often heard, "That sounds a lot like our licensed lay pastors program." Various denominations have different names for this kind of order of ministry. In a previous time, they might have been called "catechists" or "lay missionaries." Recently more professional titles have been developed, often including words like "certified" or "licensed" and some mention of lay status. The vision we hold is not of "certified lay ministers." While recognizing the value and importance of such a role in the life of denominations and in the life of many small-membership churches, we are proposing something different: laypeople who receive basic instruction in the art of worship, using their God-given gifts in service to their own or neighboring congregations, for the love of God and God's people.

While not opposed to "certified lay ministers," we have concerns about how congregations and judicatories see and use these faithful servants. First, these individuals are often paid less than ordained clergy and are offered to financially struggling congregations as a way to maintain church life. The ministry model is not transformed; it is simply made cheaper. Thus when the congregation reaches a point when it can no longer support the "certified lay minister," the members are no more prepared to take up their calling as the people of God than they were when they had a "real" minister. This situation brings up a second concern with "certified lay ministers." Without specific training in equipping the saints, a certified lay minister will likely be no more effective than an ordained minister at raising up within the congregation those whom the Spirit has gifted to plan and lead worship and to preach. Both ordained clergy and "certified lay ministers" must develop collegial leadership approaches that actively involve laypeople in the process of planning and leading worship services.

It is far too easy for gifted lay leaders in small congregations to believe that their primary purpose is to find ever new and ever more labor-intensive ways to raise the funds necessary to keep the doors open. That enterprise can consume almost all the energy in a congregation, leaving few resources for the heart of congregational life. The model we propose calls for Spirit-gifted lay leaders to become involved in the most important part of church life, the fulfillment of the church's highest calling— to worship God.

Our model does not call for one lay preacher to preach every Sunday or even every second Sunday. Experience tells us that laypeople with full-time jobs outside the congregation find preaching more than once a month to be a burden. We are aware of some lay preachers who, given the rhythm of their lives, would like to preach three Sundays in a row, and then not again for three months. Given the length of time required for a group to plan a worship service, teams of worship planners and leaders work best when they have responsibility for worship every four to six weeks. If worship is to be led every Sunday by laypeople, four to six lay preachers and 12 to 18 worship planners and leaders will be needed to share the load, since these people usually have full-time responsibilities outside the church.

Such financial questions as "Do we have to pay these folks?" are sure to arise, even when the ministry is done by lay leaders. In our experience, most lay preachers would be insulted at the suggestion that they be paid for the preaching they do in their home congregations, believing instead that they are using the gifts they have been given by God and feel privileged to do so. We have heard the comment: "When I preach in my home congregation, I never let them pay me. I have said, 'Some people teach Sunday school, some sing in the choir, and some serve on committees. I preach. But I'm no more deserving of pay than these other folks, many of whom put far more time and energy into their service than I do.'"

A second question often raised relates to the administration of the sacraments. "With no ordained clergy in place, how can the congregation celebrate the sacraments?" While baptisms usually can be planned a couple of months ahead, for a time when an ordained minister will be present, Holy Communion is a different story. There is no one best practice for celebrating the Lord's Supper.

Some faith communities have developed the practice of reserving the sacrament. This practice allows for an ordained priest to bless the elements of bread and wine, which can then be served by non-ordained people in other locations. The only challenges are ensuring that a lay leader has been trained to preside at the sacrament with understanding and grace, and that enough reserved sacrament is blessed so that trips to the closest priest do not become burdensome. Congregationalist churches, with their commitment to a strong role for local lay leaders, often have few problems with celebrating the sacraments when laypeople lead worship. Lay leaders designated as elders in these traditions are often invited to say a prayer prior to communion, even when an ordained minister is present. It may not be a tremendous leap for congregations in these traditions to have lay elders oversee the entire celebration. For example, Brethren Assemblies and nondenominational congregations whose leaders grew up in that tradition maintain that the right to initiate the breaking of the bread and the passing of the cup is open to all who are members of the church of Jesus Christ.

This leaves a middle group within the Christian tradition (Presbyterian and Reformed churches, for example) that do not allow anyone but ordained clergy to administer communion but that have not clearly developed the practice of reserving the sacrament, as have the Episcopalians (Anglicans). Adding to the challenge facing this group is a growing desire for a more frequent celebration of the Lord's Supper in the life of the worshiping community. Three ways have been developed by this middle group to deal with the question of who presides at communion:

1. The most common approach is that small congregations without settled clergy have communion infrequently, when an ordained minister is able to be present. It is not hard to understand why many small-membership churches find this custom unpalatable, as something foundational to Christian worship is missing: the sacraments. A few denominations have begun to develop the practice of reserving the sacrament, allowing congregations to celebrate the Lord's Supper on a regular basis.

2. Another approach has been to selectively ordain people to celebrate the sacraments only in their own congregations. In remote communities, or in congregations whose members use a language in worship that is not spoken by any ordained minister, one person will be given authority to administer the sacraments in that context only. While this is a creative response to the challenge, it includes a troubling aspect: authority to celebrate the sacraments is based on geography, not on a theology of ordination and the role of the laity.

3. We believe it may be prudent and faithful for congregations and denominations to explore further the meaning and practice of

ordaining, electing, designating, or installing elders. While the role of such elders has been primarily administrative, we encourage consideration of expanding that role to include worship leadership and sacramental ministry. This step might well address the needs of small congregations, but must not be seen simply as a Band-Aid measure for a particular situation. Study, prayer, and dialogue about the deeper meaning and purpose of ordination must undergird any move in this direction.

We are not naïve about the complex challenges connected with celebrating the Eucharist in the small church on a regular basis. It is one of the most difficult questions posed by the gatherings of 20 or 30 who meet regularly to worship God. There will not be a one-size-fits-all answer to this question. It is to be hoped that in the patchwork of answers, denominations will give due consideration to the profound spiritual gifts possessed by many within the small-membership churches spread across the landscape.

A NEW DAY FOR LAITY

The small-membership church is a lay-driven church. Its size makes it manageable for lay leaders to know most of what is taking place in the church. Its feeling of being like a family means that people know each other directly without the mediation of the pastor. Because of the rapid turnover of clergy, day-to-day leadership decisions tend to be made by laypeople. But that lay involvement has rarely moved into the area of worship and preaching. Given the realities of the North American church and the North American economy, lay leaders in small-membership churches will need to take on roles in worship planning and leading and in preaching. There is no way around the fact that in purely economic terms, small-membership churches need to explore models of ministry that have longer-term economic viability than present approaches. However, we propose this model not because of economics but because we believe it is a faithful way for the church to be the church.

While some lay leaders may feel as though they are being asked to do more than they signed up for, we believe that many laypeople have been waiting for the opportunity to use their gifts in meaningful ways. Some laity feel trivialized, asked to pay bills and serve tea, but not permitted to engage in the public-leadership ministry of the church they love. Others have been hesitant to step forward, fearful that they will not be able to fulfill the task they have been asked to do. With wise coaching, these individuals can develop the confidence to lead worship with wisdom and reverence. Still others are apprehensive that by moving into a leadership role, they will be seen as trying to take on power to which they are not entitled. To deal with such fears, clearly articulated permission from the lay leaders of the congregation is important for the development of teams of worship planners and leaders and the training of lay preachers. Some will never have thought of themselves in such a public role, believing that others are more competent or spiritually gifted. Reminders of God's calling unlikely people into ministry challenge people to see that God has given them unexpected gifts. Amos was a tender of fig trees and Priscilla a tent maker, but each was called by God into ministry.

Congregations benefit enormously from having gifted and trained lay worship planners and leaders in their midst. A team of people can give voice more easily to the range of experiences, concerns, and joys present in a congregation Sunday by Sunday than can a single leader. Even when they are not leading worship, team members are engaged in praise and prayer, modeling for those around them the habits of active participation in worship. Knowledgeable worshipers act as advocates for the renewal of worship, supporting the minister in the challenge of helping all who gather to discover the meaning and purpose of worship.

Even if we are wrong about the future shape of the small congregation, even if there are no economic concerns forcing small-membership churches to explore alternative models of ministry, and even if the congregation of 20 or 30 is looking ahead to seven or more years of ministry with a much-loved full-time ordained minister, we are convinced that the training of laypeople to plan and lead worship services and to preach is a right and faithful practice. This practice is not just for small churches but for all congregations regardless of their size, to fulfill their calling as a community of faith in which God's people are equipped to use the gifts of the Holy Spirit.

Ever Keep the End in View

Jim drove away from the small church, waving to a few members as he headed for home. Chores had to be done, the new lambs needed a good going-over, and the ewes would be thirsty, no doubt. Jim smiled to himself as he thought about the children's story that morning. He'd asked the youngsters "What have your parents or grandparents taught you to do?" The answers came quickly:

> *"My mother taught me how to wash dishes."*
> *"My dad taught me how to ride a bike."*
> *"My grandma helped me learn how to tie my shoes."*

But one answer made everyone take notice. Blond-haired, innocent-faced Joey had his own perspective, as usual. "My mom showed me how to pump my arm up and down to get truck drivers to honk their horns!" That brought quite a chuckle from everyone gathered—and a moment of acute embarrassment for Joey's petite mother. Jim was able to gather up all these answers and remind all the church family how important it is to teach and to learn whatever serves our highest purpose and brings us joy.

On the ride home, Jim felt that he had served a purpose and experienced great joy. He'd been hesitant at first to learn about worship and leadership. He was, after all, just a millwright and a hobby farmer. But when Pastor Cheryl had approached him and a few others to form a worship leadership team, he had decided to give it a try. He'd learned about praise, about prayer, and about preaching. He'd come to a deeper understanding of Scripture and of God's call. He'd learned to write sermons and to prepare prayers. Everything had its purpose. But more than that, Jim was discovering the joy of serving God and his church family. Jim remembered something he'd learned from his grandfather—the first question and answer of the Shorter Catechism: "What is the chief end of humankind?" Jim answered the question aloud. "Our chief end is to glorify God and enjoy him forever."

NOTES

Chapter 1 BLEST BE THE TIE THAT BINDS

1. Arlin J. Rothauge, *Sizing Up a Congregation for New Member Ministry*, available from the Episcopal Church Center, 815 Second Ave., New York, NY 10017.

2. Peter Bush, "Is bigger better, or is small more beautiful?" *Christian Week*, large church insert, spring 2003, 6.

3. For more information, see *www.smcenter.org/damien.htm*.

4. Andrew Hagen, "Learning to Pastor a Small Congregation," *Congregations*, vol. 24, no. 1, Jan.–Feb. 1998, 14.

5. David Poling-Goldenne and L. Shannon Jung, *Discovering Hope: Building Vitality in Rural Congregations* (Minneapolis: Augsburg Fortress, 2001), 106.

6. Dean R. Hoge and Jacqueline E. Wenger, *Pastors in Transition: Why Clergy Leave Local Church Ministry* (Grand Rapids: Eerdmans, 2005), 30.

Chapter 2 JESUS, WHERE'ER THY PEOPLE MEET

1. William H. Willimon and Robert L. Wilson, *Preaching and Worship in the Small Church*, Creative Leadership Series, Lyle Schaller, ed. (Nashville: Abingdon, 1980), 15.

2. Dean R. Hoge and Jacqueline E. Wenger, *Pastors in Transition: Why Clergy Leave Local Church Ministry* (Grand Rapids: Eerdmans, 2005), 95.

3. Michael Lindvall, *The Good News from North Haven* (New York: Crossroads, 2002), 94.

4. David R. Ray, *Wonderful Worship in Smaller Churches*, (Cleveland: Pilgrim Press, 2000), v.

5. Ibid.

Chapter 3 TO GOD BE THE GLORY

1. Cynthia Woolever and Deborah Bruce, *Beyond the Ordinary: Ten Strengths of U.S. Congregations* (Louisville: Westminster John Knox, 2004), 31.

2. Michael Lindvall in a question and answer session after his presentation, "Teaching about Worship: Weekly Practices at Not Being God," at Symposium on Worship and the Arts, Calvin Institute of Christian Worship, January 2005.

3. Corinne Ware, *Discover Your Spiritual Type: A Guide to Individual and Congregational Growth* (Bethesda: Alban Institute, 1995).

4. "Turn! Turn! Turn!," music and words by Pete Seeger, adapted from Ecclesiastes 3:1-8.

5. John Stott, *I Believe in Preaching*; U.S. title, *Between Two Worlds* (London: Hodder and Stoughton, 1982), 135-179.

6. *Worship Sourcebook* (Grand Rapids: Calvin Institute of Christian Worship; Faith Alive Christian Resources: A Ministry of CRC Publications; and Baker Books, 2004). This resource can be ordered through the Web site *www.FaithAliveResources.org* or by calling the toll-free number (800) 333-8300.

7. From *Worship Sourcebook*, 692-693; copyright © CRC Publications, used by permission. Originally published in *A Child Shall Lead: Children in Worship;* copyright © 1999 Choristers Guild. All rights reserved. Used by permission.

8. Karla Wubbenhorst, "The Ordinances," *The Presbyterian College Newsletter* 20, no. 2 (Fall 2004): 4.

Chapter 4 RIDE ON, RIDE ON

1. Robert L. Wilson, *The Multi-Church Parish*, Creative Leadership Series, Lyle Schaller, series ed. (Nashville, Abingdon, 1989), 56.

2. David Cutts, *Worship in Small Congregations* (Bramcote, Nottingham: Grove Books Ltd., 1989), 20 (footnote).

3. Dietrich Bonhoeffer, *Life Together*, trans. by John W. Doberstein, (New York: Harper & Row, 1954), 29-30.

4. Wilson, *Multi-Church Parish*, 91, 88.

Chapter 5 SAVIOR, LIKE A SHEPHERD LEAD US

1. "Interim moderator" is a role assigned by a presbytery of the Presbyterian Church in Canada to an ordained minister who assists a congregation in the task of searching for a new minister and in maintaining congregational life during the vacancy. This minister usually has her or his own congregation in addition to this position.

2. Lyle Schaller, *Small Congregation, Big Potential: Ministry in the Small Membership Church* (Nashville: Abingdon, 2003), 87-88.

Chapter 6 O BREATH OF LIFE, COME SWEEPING
THROUGH US

1. Carl S. Dudley, *Making the Small Church Effective* (Nashville: Abingdon, 1978), 176 (formatting ours).

2. David R. Ray, *The Big Small Church Book* (Cleveland, Pilgrim Press, 1992), 219.

3. Loren B. Mead, "Judicatory Interventions Can Help Small Congregations," in *New Possibilities for Small Churches*, ed. Douglas Alan Walrath (New York: Pilgrim Press, 1983), 87.

4. Shannon Jung, et al., *Rural Ministry: The Shape of the Renewal to Come* (Nashville: Abingdon, 1998), 9-10.

5. Summarized and adapted from "What Congregations Need from Middle Judicatories," *Alban Weekly* (free-subscription e-mail newsletter), no. 46, "Middle Judicatories," June 6, 2005; from Loren B. Mead, *Transforming Congregations for the Future* (Bethesda: Alban Institute, 1994).